BUILDING YOUR SPIRITUAL RESUME

JOHNNY M. HUNT

3H Publishers • Woodstock, Georgia

Published by 3H Publishers, Woodstock, Georgia

Design: Ernest Pullen

Manuscript edited by Carolyn Cunningham.

Printed in the United States of America

Unless otherwise indicated, Scripture quotations in this book are from the King James Version (KJV).

Other Scripture quotations are from the Holy Bible, New International Version (NIV). Copyright © 1973, 1978, 1984, International Bible Society.

ACKNOWLEDGEMENTS

This book is dedicated to three ladies who have been used by God to shape my life.

My precious wife Janet has been the love of my life for our twenty-nine years of marriage. She is the greatest encourager a man could possibly desire.

Deanna comes next. She is my little darling and has added such meaning to my life. She has been a blessing to all four churches we have served and an absolute delight to her daddy.

Then there's Hollie - Miss Sunshine. She is a bright spot in every life she touches. She has brought much happiness to her mother and me.

These three ladies have been the strength and joy in my journey of building a spiritual resume.

CONTENTS

FOREWORD

The greatest miracles are not the miracles of glory but the miracles of grace. Indeed, Jesus turned water into wine and manifested His glory. A greater miracle (I really mean this) is when God transforms a sinner into a saint. One of these greater miracles is the man called Johnny Hunt.

There is no cost to the Almighty in the miracles of creation or even in raising the dead. He does these simply because He is God. He speaks, and it is so. At His word universes sprung into being. Jesus could look into the open mouth of the hungry grave and call Lazarus to come forth. He had to obey. Jesus did this with a word.

But when Jesus saves a soul, that is another matter. The miracles of glory are done by His word and power, but the miracle of grace requires bloody Calvary. In order to be true to His own righteous standards, the Almighty had to pay the sin debt before He could call us justified. This is why I am so thankful and thrilled to write this Foreword concerning the miracle called Johnny Hunt.

You will read of a miracle - a genuine miracle - a man heaven born, heaven bound, and heaven blessed.

The testimony of the saints is a great weapon in the hand of a holy God against Satan. The apostle John tells of how the saints overcome Satan.

"And they overcame him by the blood of the Lamb, and by

the word of their testimony; and they loved not their lives unto the death" (Revelation 12:11).

Please note carefully that a part of this formula that John gives for victory over the foe is testimony. No wonder the Bible admonishes, "Let the redeemed of the Lord say so."

Johnny Hunt is the pastor of the First Baptist Church of Woodstock, Georgia. The ministry of this dynamic church reads in some ways like the Book of Acts. The church is a joyful fellowship, charged with vision and expectancy. That fellowship has caught the spirit of their anointed pastor whose life and philosophies are recorded in this volume.

I encourage you to read this book with an open heart. Remember that this is not armchair theology. This is not fiction. This is reality, mingled with practicality. It will bless. It will burn. It will build.

Dr. Adrian Rogers, Pastor
Bellevue Baptist Church
Memphis, Tennessee

INTRODUCTION

Solomon gave us two great statements concerning our name:

"A good name is more desirable than great riches; to be esteemed is better than silver or gold" (Proverbs 22:1, NIV).

"A good name is better than precious ointment; and the day of death than the day of one's birth" (Ecclesiastes 7:1).

A good name is that which has influence and character. God can so use a good name to influence change in others. From the day one is born until the day he or she dies, there is the making of a personal testimony and the building of a spiritual resume.

Everyone has three names:
* The one your parents gave you.
* The one that others call you.
* The one you make for yourself.

Before a person gets saved, God works on you; after you are saved, He works in you; and after He works in you, He works through you. When you get saved, God deposits all of Heaven in you!

"For the Lord giveth wisdom: out of his mouth cometh knowledge and understanding. He layeth up sound wisdom for the righteous: he is a buckler to them that walk uprightly. He keepeth the paths of judgment, and preserveth the way of his saints. Then shalt thou understand righteousness, and judgment, and equity; yea, every good path. When wisdom entereth into thine heart, and knowledge is pleasant unto thy soul; Discretion shall preserve thee, understanding shall keep thee" (Proverbs 2:6-11).

God is the manufacturer; we are the distributors. This is why Paul told the church at Philippi, "work out your own salvation" (Philippians 2:12). God places His treasure deep within each Christian. His treasures are like rubies - you must dig deep to find them. Precious jewels are not found on the surface - you must excavate to unearth them. Simply going through religious exercises will not uncover the things of God. We must become "spiritual miners" and plunge into the depths of God's bounty.

It is not difficult to live the Christian life at church. This mining process starts there and continues as we walk *daily* with our Lord. If we do not walk with God *daily*, then we will likely join the ranks of the fallen - those who have lost their testimony; those who no longer carry any "spiritual credentials" on their "spiritual resume." I have pastored for twenty-three years, in that time I have observed that those who fall and lose their testimony are fortunate if they live long enough to regain it!

As we live out the truths and principles of *Building Your Spiritual Resume*, God builds into us a name that will outlast us. The testimony we leave behind will be either a lovely fragrance or a foul stench. God help us to so assimilate these truths that value may be added to others.

Out of the Poolroom

Occasionally, someone will stop me and ask: "Johnny, do you think a person can be saved and not changed?" I always tell them I have an opinion but that my opinion really doesn't matter. However, when God has an opinion, it really does matter. The Bible says, "If any man be in Christ, he is a new creature: old things are passed away; behold, all things are become new" (2 Corinthians 5:17).

Jesus Christ is in the life-changing business. He changed Saul of Tarsus; He changed Simon the fisherman; He changed Matthew, the tax collector; He even changed a man who was possessed with many demons! I would like to share with you my personal experience with the living God and how He changed my life forever. Making a testimony starts with having one! I had to come to a saving knowledge of the Lord Jesus Christ first and foremost. Then I continue in my walk and relationship with Him day by day.

The Early Years

I grew up in Wilmington, North Carolina. I was what we called the "knee baby." "The what baby?" you may ask. Where I come from, if you are the next to youngest, you're the "knee baby." I have three brothers and two sisters. My father was a heavy equipment operator; and my mom, at that time, was a housewife and mother of six. Dad was a big man - 6' 1" and 230 pounds - who worked hard all week; and when he came home, he felt he owed it to himself to drink hard all weekend. But I remember some happy times with my family in those early years. I have especially fond memories of our Christmases together.

We were living in a little government project called Nesby Courts which I recall vividly. Early one morning my father came into my bedroom - as he had done with the rest of my brothers and sisters. Reaching over, he gave me a kiss on the cheek and told me "goodbye." He had decided to divorce my mother and move to Kentucky.

Hard Times at Home
As a result of Dad leaving, Mom was forced to go to work. She was a wonderful provider, working all day in the factory and then at a second job in a restaurant at night. To this day I make every attempt to be kind to waitresses because I see my mother in every one of those dear people. In fact, nothing aggravates me more than to eat out with someone who is rude to the person waiting on us. Whether I get good service or not, I always make it a point to leave a gracious tip. My mom always did her best to raise us. I can honestly say I never went hungry and was deprived of very little.

I can remember how I used to resent my dad for leaving us all alone there in that tiny project with six children and Mom having to work two jobs. After becoming a minister, I occasionally talked about how I resented him. Then one night a sweet lady in my congregation came up to me and said, "You know, Johnny, when you have the opportunity, I'd like to sit down with you and tell you about an alcoholic father that didn't leave. In a way, you ought to be thanking God that yours did." I had never thought about it from that perspective. So, in a way, I guess I am kind of grateful - now that I understand how he abused my mom and lost his temper often with his children.

A Rebellious Child

As a young boy, I loved school and did the best work I could. One of my teachers, Miss Harmon, said I was one of the finest students in the eighth grade. She was a wonderful lady who had a deep desire to positively influence her students. However, as I grew into my teenage years, I became rebellious and disobedient.

While attending New Hanover High School, one of my teachers was absent and the substitute who was called in that day was none other than Miss Harmon! She immediately recognized me and began to tell the class what an excellent student I was. I wish you could have seen the expressions of my classmates. *Surely, she must be mistaken!* they thought. She went on to tell them that I was one of her finest students and that if she had a question she was confident I would know the answer. The truth was, however, that now I didn't have a clue as to what she was talking about. Years had passed since I had been Miss Harmon's prize student, and she had no way of knowing that my heavy use of alcohol changed every area of my life.

In the project where we lived, parties were held in the recreation building on Friday and Saturday evenings. My older

brother Buddy would go to the dance with his friends just to
hang out and get drunk. I thought: *Boy, they are so cool!* I
remember sneaking into the bushes behind the building
where they hid their whiskey; and one night at the impres-
sionable age of eleven, I experienced what it meant to be
drunk.

The next morning my brother Norman who is now also a
Baptist preacher, came into my room and sprayed air fresh-
ener all over me. I looked up at him and asked, "Norman,
what in the world are you doing?" "Johnny," he answered,
"you came in last night and puked all over yourself. I was
spraying you because the odor is all through the house!"

They say that if you ever drink to the point where you don't
remember opening the bottle, you're probably an alcoholic.
From that point on, as an eleven-year-old boy, I came home
on a regular basis not remembering where I'd been.

Sunset Park Poolroom
When I was about fourteen, I wanted more than anything in
the world to be able to attend a little place called Sunset Park
Poolroom. All my older buddies went there. Donald Pope,
another Baptist minister and a dear friend to this day, used
to hang out there. Man, I thought he was cool! What fun it
would be to go there and hang out with him and all the other
guys.

Then a friend of mine did me a seemingly great favor. He
found a driver's license of a person who was sixteen years old
with green eyes and brown hair. The height and weight listed were close to my own. Because my eyes are brown, I
would never look anyone in the eye who was checking my

ID. It also was to my advantage that pictures were not placed on driver's licenses in those days. So, at age fourteen, I became a regular at Sunset Park Poolroom.

My mom would give me lunch money and send me off to school. I'd go straight to the poolroom and ask, "How long can I play for ninety cents?" If no one was there, the owner would say, "Just go on back in the corner and find a table. If it starts getting crowded, I'll take you off." So for the next five years of my life I played pool - sometimes for as long as eight hours a day.

Years later when I became the chaplain of a local high school football team, some of the players occasionally asked, "Pastor Hunt, what did you play when you were in high school?" "Nine ball," I replied. It sounds funny, but it's true. I had no athletic ability whatsoever. You don't learn much in a pool hall - except how to swing a pool stick when a brawl breaks out. Nevertheless, that's where I spent most of my high school days. As a teenage student of the pool hall, I learned how to play position pool, straight pool and in tournaments. I habitually drank and cursed and gambled for large sums of money.

High School Dropout
In the ninth grade, I skipped more days of school than I attended. The truant officer finally found me, and I was put on probation. To my shame, I was suspended from school more times than I care to remember. But even as a young fifteen or sixteen-year-old, I understood there was no purpose and no direction in my life.

When I turned sixteen, the first thing I did was get my dri-

ver's license. The second thing I did was quit school. Why?
Because they told me I had to give an oral book report. Back
in those days, I was extremely shy. I couldn't sleep at night
and I couldn't eat, thinking about standing before a crowd of
people and speaking. I was so terrified of the idea that I was
willing to quit school before I'd stand before a group and give
a report. So I quit, and it was all downhill from there.

As a high school dropout, I had an abundance of free time.
So the owner of the poolroom hired me; and I became the
manager of Sunset Park Poolroom, spending most of my
days and evenings there.

The Accident
One result of hanging around the poolroom was that I had
very little money. My sister Mary had a good job and a good
car and was gracious enough to let me drive it on the weekends or whenever I had a date.

One night I went with some buddies to the drive-in. Being
heavily under the influence, we got into a little scuffle there.
Not liking the way things turned out, I went home with a
friend of mine and got a shotgun. I put it in the back of the
car and headed back to the drive-in with every intention of
killing the guy I felt had done me wrong.

On the way there, I ran off the right side of the road. I jerked
the wheel back, and the car went into a spin. We spun several times across the median. When we finally stopped, the
car was upside down, facing the traffic. I was hanging out of
the car, having been dragged down the road. I was hoping I
would die in that accident because I was scared to death to
face my sister. She had told me before I left: "You better not

drink. And if you do and you wreck my car, I'll kill you!" One of the most frightening moments ever in my life was having to tell my sister - as she came to the hospital - and then afterwards as they put me in jail for the night - that I had totaled her car.

An Ugly Car and a Pretty Girl

I continued to run the poolroom from the age of sixteen until about nineteen. During that time, I got another job working at a place called Jacobi Hardware. By then (1969) I had a car of my own - a beat-up, old '59 Chevrolet. It was so ugly I wouldn't drive it anywhere for fear I'd see someone I knew! If anyone asked me if I had a car, I would tell them "no" because I was too embarrassed to be seen in it. I was so ashamed of that car I had a friend of mine named Don take me home every day after work.

One day Don was driving me home; and he said, "I'm kind of in a hurry today, John. If you don't mind, could I just let you off at Carolina Beach Road? You could cut right through to your apartments, couldn't you?" I told him I didn't mind, so he let me off; and I began walking down the road toward home. Just as I was about to cut through to the apartments, at 319 Bordeaux Avenue, I spotted a cute, little girl about 5' 2" outside her house, twirling her baton. The closer I got, the prettier she looked.

The next day I decided it was silly for Don to go so far out of his way just to take me home! "Why don't you just let me off at Bordeaux Avenue?" I suggested. So from then on, he dropped me off there; and I walked by that same house. I wasn't even a Christian yet; but I remember praying: "If there is a God in Heaven, please let her be out there!" And sure enough, every day she would be outside, twirling her baton.

That cute, little 5' 2" baton twirler is now my wife Janet. And what I didn't know at that time was that every day when she was outside twirling her baton, she was really waiting for me to walk by! We started seeing each other and immediately fell in love. Finally, after a lengthy courtship of six months, I asked her to marry me. And on November 21, 1970, Janet became my bride.

Not long after that, our marriage was in serious trouble. I was spending most of my weekends at the bar, managing the poolroom during the week and also hanging around Jacobi Hardware. That's when Janet began to talk to me about going to church.

My wife grew up in a Presbyterian church under the influence of her grandmother Selma Allen, one of the godliest ladies I've ever known. Janet used to call and plead with me to go to church. It really impressed me how much she wanted me to attend. So about every two months or so, she would ask on Saturday night: "Can we go to church tomorrow?" "Let's wait and see in the morning," I would reply. But in the morning, I would act like I was so tired I couldn't get out of bed. She would say: "Let's go to church, honey." And I would groan: "Boy, I don't know what's wrong with me. I just feel nauseous! Let's go some other time." I would do anything and everything I could to keep from going to church.

N. W. Pridgen
Then a fellow by the name of N. W. Pridgen began to come to

the hardware store where I worked. He was a very simple man who lived on Shipyard Boulevard - right down the road from Long Leaf Baptist Church in Wilmington. Regardless of what our conversation would be, Mr. Pridgen would never leave the store without saying: "You know, Johnny, I wish you would come to church with me sometime. I'm a member of Long Leaf Baptist Church." And I would always tell him: "Thank you for inviting me, but I'm a faithful attendant down at the Presbyterian church." What that really meant was that I went at Easter and Christmas.

Let me just stop here to say: You may be reading this book right now, and the bottom line for you is that you are lost and on your way to Hell. You've been hiding behind the disguise of a church membership somewhere; but you're just as lost as a goose, and you know you'd go to Hell if you died this instant. That was my attitude back there at the hardware

You may be reading this book right now, and the bottom line for you is that you are lost and on your way to Hell. You've been hiding behind the disguise of a church membership somewhere; but you're just as lost as a goose, and you know you'd go to Hell if you died this instant.

store. I would tell him: "Listen, I'm a good old Presbyterian boy. I appreciate you asking, but I'm going to keep going with my wife over at her church." But Mr. Pridgen would always come back. And every time he did, he'd invite me to church.

A Changed Life

One day Mr. Pridgen asked me: "Johnny, do you know an old boy that hangs around the poolroom by the name of Drew Todd?"

"Yeah, I know Drew."

"Did you hear what happened to him last week?"

"No, I haven't seen him," I said. "He used to hang around the poolroom all the time."

"Well," he said, "Drew got saved."

Now I didn't know what it meant to "get saved." I thought that people simply decided whether or not to be religious, and I had chosen not to be. I had made up my mind that I wouldn't go to church. Apparently, Drew had decided that he would.

But let me tell you what I remembered about Drew. In the early seventies, some self-proclaimed prophetess had said the world was going to come to an end on Saturday night. I remembered Drew standing out in front of the poolroom, shaking his fist at the sky and saying, "If there's a God in Heaven, strike me dead!" And now I'm hearing that Drew is going over to the Baptist church and that God has changed his life!

Long Leaf Baptist Church

Week after week N.W., as I was now calling him, would come in; and before he would leave, he would always say: "Well, you know what I'm going to ask you, don't you?" And I sure did. I had heard it so many times it sounded to me like a recording on Dial-A-Devotion! But in November of 1972, I finally told my wife: "If you're going to keep hounding me about church, let's just get up and go to the Baptist church that's right down the street from our house." We drove two blocks to Long Leaf Baptist Church; and when we went in, I asked one of the men if N. W. Pridgen was there. And on the very day that I went, Mr. Pridgen was not there! He came back in the store the next week and said, "I want you to come to church with me." I told him: "I went the other day, and you weren't there!"

Marian Bennett, the woman who later became my church secretary in Wilmington, told me that she remembered the first day Janet and I came to church. She punched her husband Mitchell and said, "Would you look back there? There's a fine-looking Christian couple!" Isn't it amazing how we can disguise ourselves to look like we're on our way to Heaven?

A fellow asked me recently: "Preacher, where do you believe Judas is right now?"

I said, "The Bible teaches that Judas is in Hell."

"Well, do you think that he got saved and then got lost?"

> ### *Isn't it amazing how we can disguise ourselves to look like we're on our way to Heaven?*

"No, not at all!" I replied. "Judas was never saved. Jesus even referred to him as the 'devil.'" The fellow was shocked. "Are you saying that someone could hang around with the disciples and walk in intimacy with Jesus Christ and not be saved?" That's exactly what I'm saying! You can preach; you can give testimony; you can hold street meetings and still not be saved! So, you see, even though I looked like a fine Christian man, wearing my blue pinstripe suit to church that morning, I was lost and without God.

Deep Conviction

Then in December of 1972, after attending Long Leaf Baptist Church for several weeks, God began to bring me under deep conviction. My friend Donald Pope was in the Navy during that time. He and his wife Debbie were stationed in Norfolk, Virginia. One weekend they invited us to come up and visit them. I can remember Donald and I sitting there drinking Bloody Marys, while I was telling him the difference that God was making in my life!

"Donald," I said, "I just want you to know that I've been attending a Baptist church." He confided, "You know, I've been thinking about religion lately, too." "Man, it's wonderful," I said. "It's a great feeling to go to church!"

By the way, do you know that a lot of people are going to go to Hell with "good feelings" because they have never been saved? I was just as lost at Long Leaf Baptist Church as I had been hanging around the poolroom.

> ## Do you know that a lot of people are going to go to Hell with "good feelings?"

Then something began to happen in my life. I would go to church and everything would be fine as long as the sermon was being preached or somebody was singing. But then the preacher would say: "We're going to stand together in a moment and sing an invitation hymn." I don't know what would happen to me, but I would begin to weep. Someone told me - and now I understand after being a Christian - that it was conviction.

The Lord Jesus says when the Holy Spirit - the *parakletos,* the Comforter - comes, He will convict the world of sin, righteousness and judgment to come. (John 16:7-11) That means the Holy Spirit will expose your need for Jesus Christ. I was sitting in that worship service, and God was exposing my need.

Now let me just catch you up on what was happening in my life up to that point. I used to ride by the church in my red '67 GTO and say to my wife: "Do you see those guys out in front of the church? Half of them hang out at the poolroom and gamble with me. And look at them! You see the cigarettes in their hands?"

But do you know what? When the Holy Spirit convicts you of sin, you don't look at other people's faults anymore - you look at your own. You no longer measure yourself by somebody at the church; you measure yourself by Jesus Christ, the sinless, perfect, holy Son of God. And so the Holy Spirit began to convict me of my sin.

I would cry during the invitation. I call God as my witness that I had never carried a handkerchief in my back pocket as long as I lived until I started attending a Baptist church! I thought I was such a big shot, hanging around the poolroom, that I didn't want anybody to see my tears. So I'd pull that old handkerchief out, while all the heads were bowed and everybody was praying; and I'd wipe my tears, so

When the Holy Spirit convicts you of sin, you don't look at other people's faults anymore - you look at your own.

nobody would know that I had been crying. I was ashamed of the fact that I couldn't handle my emotions when God began to move on my heart.

When God Speaks, You Listen!

One cold Sunday morning in January, my wife and I got up and went to church. While we were sitting there, the same thing happened. I wish I could tell you that the preacher delivered this great sermon (he probably did) and tell you the title and the text he used. But I don't remember anything about the sermon. I only remember thinking: "Oh, God, here comes the invitation!" And when they gave it, the tears began to flood.

They stood that morning and sang:

> *Just as I am, without one plea*
> *But that thy blood was shed for me,*
> *And that thou bidd'st me come to thee,*
> *O Lamb of God, I come! I come!*[1]

As they were singing that song, I fell under conviction and was weeping. My wife noticed that I was crying. "Are you all right?" she asked.

"Yes, I'm fine."

"Well, then, what's wrong with you?" But I just told her to "shut up." You see, I didn't know what was happening in my life; and it embarrassed me for her to know that I was crying.

Debbie Joyner, a friend of mine from high school, was sitting on the other side of me. She and her husband Alfred were wonderful church people and I knew them well; but I didn't know they were Christians. I just knew they were wonderful church people! Debbie asked me: "Johnny, would you like to go forward and be saved this morning?" Nobody had ever personally asked me this question; and to be honest, everything in my heart wanted to say "yes." But my pride said, "Not today."

After the service we would normally go home just for a moment and then we'd make our way forty-five miles north to the Holly Ridge Drag Strip where I raced my GTO on Sunday afternoons. But that day I said, "You know, I don't think I want to go to the drag strip today. Why don't we hang around the house and go back to church tonight?" Now I had never been to an evening worship service in my entire life. I had never even attended a revival service. Janet could hardly believe it. "You want to go back to church tonight?"

"Yeah, you know the preacher was talking about me this morning," I answered. She thought I meant I had been offended and wouldn't go back anymore. So she said, "Oh, Johnny, he wasn't talking about you!" But I disagreed.

"During the invitation," I told her, "the preacher said, 'There's a young man here, and God's dealing with him. We need to pray that God will save him. Let's just join together and pray that God will bring him back and save him tonight.'

Janet, he was talking about me."

"Oh, no," she assured me, "he wasn't talking about you!" But isn't it amazing when God speaks to you, it doesn't matter what anybody else says; you know He's talking to you! And God was speaking to my heart that day.

> *But isn't it amazing when God speaks to you, it doesn't matter what anybody else says; you know He's talking to you!*

'Tell Him I Want to be Saved'

Then I said to Janet, "Did you know that somebody once came up to me and offered me some speed? 'This will keep you awake,' he said, 'and you can drink yourself sober!' And I said, 'Man, give me one!' Somebody else said, 'Drink this, and it will make you act like these guys!' And I said, 'Boy, give me one!' It's amazing what I have allowed to come into my life on faith, never knowing for sure until I took it in. Janet, if Jesus Christ can change my life - and I sure feel that I need it - then I am willing to give my heart and life to Him."

And it was then that my wife said, "Well, you know, honey, there's something that I've never shared with you. Just before I started dating you, I was going to a little revival. God moved on my heart, and I fell under deep conviction. I want you to know that I know I am saved."

"You are?" I said. "Well then, since you're saved, I want you to do me a favor. I want you to go to church tonight; and when the invitation is given, I want you to go down and tell that preacher that I want to be saved!"

"No!"

"Come on! You know how timid and shy I am! I am not going to walk that aisle in front of all those people. I just can't do it. I'm too scared! Just go on down and tell him."

"No, you've got to go tell him yourself."

"No, I can't go tell him."

> ## "If Jesus Christ can change my life - and I sure feel that I need it - then I am willing to give my heart and life to Him."

"Well, if you want to get saved bad enough, you'll go and tell him!" This was before we knew anything about soul-winning or bringing people to Jesus Christ. All afternoon I waited with nervous dread, thinking: *Oh, God! What am I going to do?*

Finally, it was time for the church service; and I pleaded with Janet: "Listen, why don't we go down together and you tell him I want to get saved?" But she still said no. "If you want to get saved, you ought to go on down by yourself."

January 7, 1973

That afternoon as I sat nervously awaiting the evening service, it snowed. It had not snowed in January in Wilmington in two years. And let's be honest, it only takes nineteen drops of rain to keep twenty Baptists out of church! But that Sunday night, it snowed again. I guess God was saving another young preacher!

I had every reason in the world not to go to church. But in my heart of hearts, I really wanted to give my life to Jesus Christ. I wanted to invite Him into my heart and give Him an opportunity to change my life if, indeed, He was the very God who could do it.

I wanted to invite Him into my heart and give Him an opportunity to change my life.

Normally, we'd walk in the church and sit near the back. But I knew I was going to be going forward that night, and I didn't want to walk a long way. So we moved up to about the third pew. A friend of mine, Roy Joyner, was sitting there. "Come on over!" he called. But I said, "No, if you don't mind, I want you to move on in!" I didn't want to have to climb over anybody. I wanted to make it as easy as I possibly could!

I sat there during that whole service with my mind consumed by the fact that when the invitation was given, I would be going forward to trust my life to Jesus Christ. I had never been much for praying; but that afternoon I had prayed: "Dear Lord, I'm going to come down tonight to trust You. I'd appreciate it if You'd help me not to cry." So that night when the invitation was given, I didn't cry. I just went down, and I told the preacher: "I want to give my heart and life to Jesus Christ." I'll never forget that moment; it's indelibly written in my heart and mind.

The preacher worked a little different with people than we

do now. He said, "Now, son, do you believe Jesus died on the cross?"

"Yes, Mr. Gibson. I believe Jesus died."

"Do you believe He died on the cross for your sins?"

"Yes, sir. I do."

"Now, are you asking Jesus to come into your life today? Is that what you want to do?"

"Yes, sir. I want Jesus Christ to come into my heart."

"Do you believe God raised Him from the dead?"

"Yes, sir."

"Since you said you want Him to come into your heart and you're coming to ask Him into your heart, do you believe He is in your heart?"

"Yes, sir. I do!"

And that night, January 7, 1973, Jesus changed my life!

Gloriously Saved!

These days someone will question whether or not you prayed the prayer just right, if you came down the aisle just right or how somebody counseled you. But my Bible tells me that God knows the heart. And God looked at the heart of Johnny Hunt when he came down that night, and He knew that I was a high school dropout and basically illiterate. I knew very little about praying. I knew nothing about God or His Word. I only knew I was lost and wanted to be saved. And that night Jesus Christ came into my life, and I was gloriously saved!

At the close of the service, the preacher called me to the front. "We're going to ask these who have gotten saved to stand here, so the church can come by and give them the right hand of fellowship and encourage them in their decision."

I remember people coming - some of them I knew by name. Libb Lyles came by. I remember seeing her in the choir and thinking: *She looks at me the whole time I'm here.* I felt so nervous - like she was just staring at me when I was crying. She came by and said, "Johnny, I've been praying for you for weeks!" Another little lady named Mrs. Carol said the same thing: "I've been praying for you for weeks!"

A New Creation

By the time the service was over, the ground had been totally covered with snow. The windshields on all the cars in the parking lot were hidden beneath a fine, white layer. I remembered I had a can of defogger in my car, so I spent the next hour scraping snow and ice off windshields for all the ladies in the church. God changed me! No longer was I self-centered - worried about getting home, worried about myself. I wanted to do something to help somebody else. I just felt different all over.

And I didn't know you weren't supposed to tell everybody! I went to work the next day and told Abraham Solomon, the Jewish man who I worked for: "Mr. Solomon! Mr. Solomon! Guess what happened? Last night Jesus saved me!" Now I call the Lord Jesus as my witness, I didn't know what a Jew was. I thought it was a person who had been nicknamed that for trying to "jew" you! I'd never read the Old Testament

- or any other part of the Bible for that matter. I didn't know anything about Abraham and Moses and Jacob. So when Nathan Jacobi, the owner of the hardware store, came in, I said to him: "Nathan! Nathan! Guess what? Jesus changed my life!"

For about a week, I was so excited that I was telling everybody I met how Jesus changed my life. I'd be shaking a gallon of paint at the hardware store and say to the customer: "Hey, guess what happened to me Sunday night? I got saved!" And I felt like I wasn't telling enough people! So I went out and bought some blue jeans and some little stickers that said: "Jesus Died for Me" and "Jesus Loves Me," and I put them all over my pants. There I was - working for Jews, bragging on Jesus, telling them how the Son of God changed my life!

'Home' Missions

Believe it or not, I never liked church until I got saved. Before, Janet used to beg me to go to church; and now she couldn't get me to stay home! Jesus changed my "want to" toward church. So I went home and told my whole family how Jesus changed my life. "Momma, Momma! Guess what?

Jesus changed my "want to" toward church.

Jesus changed my life!" She said, "Now, son, just tell me what happened." So I told her: "You know how I used to drink liquor all the time and go out and get drunk and get in fights? Momma, I don't ever want to drink anymore! I don't want to go to the poolroom anymore. I don't want to gamble.

Momma, all I want to do is live for Jesus!"

My brother Norman said, "Don't come talking that stuff to me! When I went to church, I used to talk to you about it and you wouldn't go." "But, Norman," I said, "I'm not talking about going to church. I'm talking about being saved. I'm changed, Norman, really changed!"

I have another brother Freddy who is 6' 4" and used to be a boxer. He came home one night and said, "You know what they're saying about you at the poolroom? They're saying that Johnny Hunt got religion, and now he thinks he's better than everybody else."

"Oh, Freddy, that's just not true!" I said.

"Well, Johnny, you talk about how much you love Jesus and love everybody."

"I do! I love Rex and Randy and Donald. I love all those guys!"

"Well, it seems to me if you loved all of them so much, you'd go up to the poolroom and tell them."

"But, Freddy, you don't understand. Jesus saved me from that lifestyle!"

Do you know that if you check your Bible, you'll find that Jesus spent more time around places like the pool hall than He did at the church? I didn't know that - not at that time. And so I refused to go.

Back in the Hood
Then God did something again that He had done before I got saved. He put me under conviction. One night I told Janet:

"I'm going to go out and talk to all my friends about Jesus tonight." "Where are you going?" she asked. "I'll tell you when I get home!" I said and walked out the door.

My first stop was at Buddy's barber shop. Buddy had a filthy mouth. If you know anything about hanging around a poolroom and the vocabulary you pick up, you can imagine that I had a filthy mouth too! It kept me in trouble. The well-known British preacher of the eighteenth century, Charles Spurgeon used to say: "When Jesus Christ came into my life, I lost eighty percent of my vocabulary!" I can really identify with that statement. Jesus literally changed my tongue. Now whenever anybody asks me: "Do you ever speak in tongues?" I tell them I've been speaking in tongues ever since I got saved! Anyway, when I met Jesus, I didn't like cussing anymore; so I found a Christian barber and stopped going to Buddy. Now I was back to tell him how Jesus had changed me.

"When Jesus Christ came into my life, I lost eighty percent of my vocabulary!"

"Buddy," I said, "I just wanted to tell you something."

"I already heard," he said. "You got religion."

"No, I didn't get religion, Buddy. I got Jesus! He changed my life."

After I left Buddy, I went over to the Red Fox Saloon where I used to drink. My friend Ray was managing the poolroom there. I'll never forget that when I walked in, Ray was playing with a cap pistol. I said, "Ray, I just want to tell you the reason I haven't been coming to the saloon on the weekends.

Jesus changed my life! And Ray, man, I don't drink anymore;
I don't cuss anymore; I quit smoking - He's just changed my
life! Man, I'm living for Jesus!" And as I was sharing my testimony with him, Ray placed that little cap pistol to his cheek
and caught his tears, hoping that I wouldn't see him crying.

Return to Sunset Park

But then I had to make the biggest step of all. I went down
to Sunset Park Poolroom. This is the place where Willie
Mosconi used to play. Fairmont Kid was known as one of the
greatest position pool players there. Also I managed that
poolroom myself for three or four years. I had been hanging
around there since I was fourteen, and now I was a twenty-
year-old man whose life Jesus Christ had changed.

I walked in and went straight up to the poolroom owner. "I
owe you an apology. I've not even been back here to official-
ly quit my job, but I guess you've heard."

"Yes, son, I'm proud of you. I heard you got religion and
joined the church."

"No, it's not just joining the church. You see, Jesus Christ
changed my life!"

"You know my wife, don't you?" he asked.

"Yes sir."

"You know, we've been talking about God lately. I wonder if
you can come by my house tomorrow night and tell us exactly what Jesus has done in your heart." Now, remember, I was
a brand new Christian. I didn't know how to quote verses of
Scripture or anything. But I said, "I'll be there tomorrow
night at six!"

Soul-Winner

I went home and called Alfred Joyner. He was a soul-winner that had been taking me witnessing. "Alfred," I said, "I think my ex-boss wants to get saved! We need to go over there and get him saved tomorrow night at six!" So Alfred agreed to meet me at my house, and from there we would go witnesssing at six.

About a quarter of six, he called and said, "I've got to work overtime, I can't go." Well, I couldn't go by myself; so I got on the phone and called the poolroom owner, "Listen," I said, "I just want to tell you that I can't come tonight. I've had something to happen, and I'm just not going to be able to go up there and share with you. Maybe I'll come tomorrow night."

I called Alfred the next night; and he said, "Man, I hate to tell you this; but I've got to work over again." I thought: *What am I going to do, Lord?*

Well, when I got saved, they gave me a Soul-Winner's New Testament. You could open it to the front page; and it would have written there: "If you want to tell somebody how to be saved, turn to page 283." And when you turned to that page, it would have a particular passage of Scripture underlined in red; so it was easy to find. Then at the bottom, it would instruct you: "Now ask them this question, and turn over two pages."

So I went to the poolroom owner's house that night and opened up my Soul-Winners's New Testament; and it directed me to Romans 3:23: "For all have sinned, and come short of the glory of God." Then: "Turn to the right two pages." So I flipped it on over and said, "Everyone has sinned and no

one is righteous. Do you realize you're a sinner?" I was reading it from the bottom of the page. He said, "Yes, I do."

Then I told them: "Now look at this. The Bible says in
Romans 6:23, 'The wages of sin is *death*....' Now this word
death here (I was a preacher even back then!) means spiritual separation from God. That means you'll go to Hell if you
don't ever get saved. Do you know you're going to Hell if you
don't get saved?"

"Yeah."

I looked at his wife and asked, "Do you know that too?"

"I sure do," she replied.

Then I turned over to Romans 5:8 and read: "But God com-
mendeth his love toward us, in that, while we were yet sin-
ners, Christ died for us." "Do you know that when Jesus died
on the cross, He died for you?"

"That's exactly right" was his answer.

"Now look at this good news. The Bible says in Romans 10:9:
'...if thou shalt confess with thy mouth the Lord Jesus, and
shalt believe in thine heart that God hath raised him from
the dead, thou shalt be saved.' Now listen to *this* one, folks -
it's the greatest promise in the Bible! Romans 10:13: `For
whosoever shall call upon the name of the Lord shall be
saved.' Do you believe if you called on the name of the Lord
Jesus, He'd hear you and forgive you?"

"I do."

"Would you like to get down on your knees and ask Jesus
Christ to come into your heart and save you?"

"That's exactly what we want to do!" So there I was - a young boy who had just gotten saved, down on his knees, praying with this dear couple, owners of the poolroom I used to manage. And that night the two of them together asked Jesus Christ to come into their hearts!

The next morning we went over to Sunset Park Poolroom and put a "for sale" sign on the front door. We wrote on it: "Going out of business." We advertised in the newspaper and sold every piece individually, so we could close that old hell hole down. Remember now, this was one of the most popular poolrooms in North Carolina! We closed it down when the owner got saved, and we baptized him at Long Leaf Baptist Church. He later became a deacon and an usher there. Someone recently asked me: "What does he do for a living now?" He bought a Tom's peanut truck and started selling peanuts.

The Talk of the Town

I spent every weekend during those days sharing my testimony with anybody who would listen. They even heard about it down at the Presbyterian church. The preacher called me up one day and told me: "Everybody in town is talking about you. They're saying that everywhere you go you're preaching and telling people how you've been changed." And it was true. People would come into the hardware store and say, "You sound like a preacher!" I sort of liked that!

One day the Presbyterian church called and invited me to speak at one of their family night suppers. "There will be more people here than there are all month," they said.

"Would you come and tell them what happened to you?" So I recruited some people from my church that could sing, and we went down to the Presbyterian church. We got around a piano and sang "I Wish We'd All Been Ready." It was a song about how time had passed and people had gone to Hell and we wish we had all been ready. I got up afterwards and told how Jesus had changed my life.

Now I was not a preacher back then, so I didn't know how to give an invitation. But this is what I said: "If you want what I got, come on down!" And they did! Both of my wife's cousins and several men came down, weeping before God and wanting to be saved. We didn't know what to do with them! I was up there saying, "Come on down! Come on down!" And they were coming down.

"If you want what I got, come on down!"

The elders of the church took them to a back room for counseling. They approached me after the service and said, "Brother Johnny, they're back there in that back room wanting to get what you got. Would you go back there and tell them how to get it?" I went back there and asked them: "Y'all want Jesus to come into your heart?" I opened my Bible to Romans 10:13: "...whosoever shall call upon the name of the Lord shall be saved." And that night they called upon the name of the Lord: and they, too, invited Jesus Christ into their hearts.

Prayer for a Mother
It became a great desire of mine to know if my mother was

saved or not. When I began to talk to my mom about it, she would tell me: "Son, when you were a little boy, we lived in Detroit, Michigan. During that time, I went to a Baptist church. And, son, I know as well as I'm breathing right now that Jesus changed my life."

"Well, Mom," I said to her, "then I want you to come to church with me." I didn't know why, but my mom was a little hard-hearted towards the idea. She had come up pretty tough, and she just would not go to church with me.

But there was a lady named Lila Todd; and she used to say to my mother: "You know, if I had a son that had been as radically changed as yours, I'd go sit with him at church. I'd be there to support him. He used to hang around the poolroom. He used to stay in trouble with the law. And now he's living for God! Bessie, if you would go there, it would really make a difference in your son's life." Then one evening my mom called me and said, "I'll go to church with you this Sunday night." True to her word, that Sunday night she went. And I prayed for her.

Now I was the type of guy who would get in there first and whisper to everybody: "My mom's here! Pray! My mom's here! Pray!" And everybody would pray.

That night the choir sang "O Why Not Tonight?":

Dear sinner, harden not your heart.
Be saved, O why not tonight?[2]

That Sunday evening my momma came forward and got right with Jesus. And for the next few years, she really lived for God.

Full Circle

Little did I know at that time that God was going to call me to preach. But He did, and I went off to Gardner-Webb College. I spent three and a half years there, and *immediately* God put me in a pastorate. I pastored the entire time at Lavonia Baptist Church in Gafney, South Carolina. From there I went to Southeastern Baptist Theological Seminary where I pastored Falls Baptist Church.

And then, after being in school for six and a half years and serving as a pastor almost as long, I got a call from Long Leaf Baptist Church, the very same church that I had gotten saved in. They said, "Johnny, we believe God wants you to be the pastor back in your hometown."

The church was about to close its doors. They were running less than ninety in Sunday School. They had an auditorium they had just built to seat over 500. Now they couldn't pay their bills. They couldn't even pay the preacher's salary. And now they were asking me if I'd consider becoming their pastor!

I didn't even have to think about it. I immediately resigned my church and became the pastor of the very church that God had saved me in, and God used me in that town to be able to touch my family and my friends and see them come to know Jesus Christ.

'Jesus Is in the Life-Changing Business!'

What I'm trying to communicate in this brief testimony is that, from the poolroom to the pulpit, what really happened to me is *Jesus Christ changed my life*. It was a simple, child-like experience. I simply believed with all my heart that on the cross, two thousand years ago, Jesus really died. They took Him down off the cross, wrapped His body, and placed Him in a borrowed tomb. And for three days, the Lord Jesus Christ was literally dead and buried..

But on the third day, early in the morning, Jesus, the living Son of God, rose from the dead! He sent the Holy Spirit of God into this world to convict our hearts of our sin and our need for Him. And He sent the Word of God to show us the way to Heaven when we die. So now it is my mission to tell everyone the message that what Jesus did for me, He will do for you! Every sermon I preach is integrated with the fact that *Jesus is in the life-changing business.*

A Simple Invitation

Maybe you are reading this book right now, and you have come to a place in your life where you feel that something is missing. Maybe your situation is similar to what mine was; maybe it's not. But you still can't help wondering: "Is he right? Can Jesus really change my life the way He changed Johnny Hunt's?"

If you would like Jesus to come into your heart, it's as easy as asking. It doesn't matter who you are or what you've done, God is ready and willing to save you and forgive your sin.

> ## *It doesn't matter who you are or what you've done, God is ready and willing to save you and forgive your sin.*

Remember what Romans 10:13 says: "*Whosoever* shall call upon the name of the Lord *shall be saved.*" That "whosoever" is you! Wherever you are, whatever you are doing, just stop right now and tell Him you want to be saved. Maybe you're not sure what to say. If that's your case, you can pray this prayer:

> *Dear Lord Jesus,*
>
> *I admit that I'm a sinner. I know that I am lost and going to Hell without You.*
>
> *I am asking You now, Jesus, to please come into my heart, forgive me of my sins and change me the way You changed Johnny Hunt. Thank You for saving me, Jesus. Thank You that I know I am saved and that You have a place for me in Heaven when I die. Now help me to live my life for You, Jesus. And help me to tell everyone I know what You have done for me. In Jesus' Name, Amen.*

If you prayed this prayer and meant it with all your heart, *you are saved!* But that is only the beginning. There is a whole life ahead of you, a life of learning more about Jesus. You can start by finding a Bible-believing church where the Word of God is taught, and other Christians will encourage you in your new faith. Read the Bible every day. Take time daily to talk with God in prayer.

The Making of a Testimony

The wisest man who ever lived was Solomon. He penned a truth around three thousand years ago that still rings true today: "A good name is more desirable than great riches, to be esteemed is better than silver or gold" (Proverbs 22:1, NIV). The millenniums have revealed the validity and accuracy of this proverb. This nugget of wisdom is certainly true in the Christian community, but its echo is heard all throughout society. A good testimony is desired in our communities, the business world, civic organizations, our schools, etc. Consider the following examples:

- Every family desires good neighbors with much character.
- Parents want their child's teacher to be above reproach.
- Every business longs for employees to have a good reputation.
- Every follower desires to be led by a person of integrity.

Webster's dictionary defines a testimony as "supporting evidence: proof." The supporting evidence of our lives gives proof to the testimony we have with others. Our lives produce either good evidence or poor evidence. This evidence then shapes our personal testimony.

How important is a testimony? It is the only real possession you have! Consider these three facts about how your testimony testifies:

It is how people view you.

People see you through the window of your reputation. You provide them a clean, shining window to see you through; or you supply a dirty window through which they must view your life. Many times someone will tell me something negative about a person who I know to be of much character. Because I view this person through a "clean window," I dismiss the statement as being exaggerated or altogether untrue. This negative statement then provides me a "dirty window" which I view the person who made the inappropriate, negative remark.

It renders you powerful or powerless.

Booker T. Washington once said, "Character is power." Character gives you influence. How can you influence someone who does not trust you? Many people are striving to gain power while bypassing integrity. A person who pursues integrity will have power, but the person who pursues power without integrity will be mad.

It is the only thing you will leave this world when you are gone.

You can leave money and possessions, but they will soon fade away. Yet when you leave a testimony, you leave a legacy that will last. History books have recorded the testimonies of those who have gone before us. Some, like George Washington and Abraham Lincoln, have left a good testimony that still positively impacts our nation. Others, like Benedict Arnold, the traitor, will for the centuries to come bear a disgraceful and unappreciated testimony.

The Bible records those that stood tall for the eternal cause of our Lord Jesus Christ. Many heroes of the faith, recorded in Hebrews 11, sealed their good testimony with their blood. Their testimonies have influenced people in the past, still have power today and will continue to permeate the hearts and souls of mankind until Jesus comes.

I wish I could stop there, but I must give you the "other side of the coin." While some will be respected forever, others will bear the testimony of reproach. Judas Iscariot is such a man. His testimony brings shame to his name. His "supporting evidence" is as follows:

He was a thief. John, one of his fellow disciples and traveling companions for three and a half years, had this to say about Judas:

> "Then Jesus six days before the passover came to Bethany, where Lazarus was which had been dead. There they made him a supper; and Martha served: but Lazarus was one of them that sat at the table with him. Then took Mary a pound of ointment of spikenard, very costly, and anointed the feet of Jesus, and wiped his feet with her hair: and the house was filled with the odor of the ointment. Then saith one of his disciples, Judas Iscariot, Simon's son, which should betray him, Why was not this ointment sold for three hundred pence, and given to the poor? *This he said, not that he cared for the poor; but because he was a thief,* and had the bag, and bare what was put therein." (John 12:1-6, emphasis mine)

He was a traitor. Dr. Luke pens this record of Judas' testimony that still testifies:

> "And while he (Jesus) yet spake, behold a multitude, and he that
> was called Judas, one of the twelve, went before them, and drew
> near unto Jesus to kiss him. But Jesus said unto him, Judas,
> betrayest thou the Son of man with a kiss?" (Luke 22:47-48, KJV)

Your testimony really is the only thing you leave this world,
and often it hinges on the doorframe of your choices. The
old Japanese proverb states: The reputation of a thousand
years may be determined by the conduct of one hour!

The Apostle Paul maintained a testimony that still stands as
a tall, polished trophy on the living room mantle. He was
careful not to offend in anything - lest blame be laid on the
Gospel. He was keenly sensitive that his conduct would
commend or condemn the message that he desired to share
with the entire world. Paul realized the first rule of winning
is to keep from losing. Therefore, he depended on God's
grace to commend him as a man of God even in the most difficult of situations.

In 2 Corinthians 6:4-10 Paul shares this testimony:

> "But in all things approving ourselves as the ministers of God, in
> much patience, in afflictions, in necessities, in distresses, (5) In
> stripes, in imprisonments, in tumults, in labors, in watchings, in
> fastings; (6) By pureness, by knowledge, by long-suffering, by
> kindness, by the Holy Ghost, by love unfeigned, (7) By the word of
> truth, by the power of God, by the armor of righteousness on the
> right hand and on the left, (8) By honor and dishonor, by evil
> report and good report: as deceivers, and yet true; (9) As unknown,
> and yet well-known; as dying, and, behold, we live; as chastened,
> and not killed; (10) As sorrowful, yet always rejoicing; as poor, yet
> making many rich; as having nothing, and yet possessing all
> things."

In this passage, we glean three things from the great apostle on how to build our testimony:

- The war he waged was his trial.

- The weapons he used were his tools.

- The worthiness he gained was his testimony.

Let's probe into each of these three for some additional insights on how to build our spiritual resume.

The War He Waged

Paul was a disciplined man and had endured many hardships. Notice the preposition "in" which Paul used in verses four and five. This was a war that he was "in." He was not observing it from afar; he was in the thick of the battle. To maintain a godly testimony, we must realize our need to crawl into the foxhole and persevere until the victory is secured. A good testimony does not come easy. It exacts a heavy toll on us. This is why Paul admonished young Timothy to "endure hardness as a good soldier" (2 Timothy 2:3). I am amazed at the mentality of those who suppose that victory is convenient and comfortable. The battle for your testimony will be the "fight *of* your life." But it also will be the "fight *for* your life." Therefore, Paul unveils three areas where the war will be waged in each of our lives.

A good testimony does not come easy.
It exacts a heavy toll on us.

The first battle we must wage is *emotional.* 2 Corinthians 6:4 lists four areas of emotional conflict. The first area of conflict in "approving ourselves as the ministers of God" is "much patience." Winning the emotional battle will take patience. Why? Because you will not always feel like doing what you know you should. You will recall that God had led the Israelites out of Egypt after four centuries of bondage. In Exodus 14 He opened up the Red Sea so that the Jews could walk across on dry ground and then drowned all of Pharaoh's army with the same waters that He parted. In Exodus 15 the children of Israel broke out into singing and praising God. Three days later they came to Marah and found only bitter water to drink. Marah means "bitter." And true to its name, the Israelites became bitter and complained against Moses and cried unto the Lord. The Lord then showed Moses a tree and told him to cast it into the bitter waters and the water would be made sweet.

Winning the emotional battle will take

patience. Why? Because you will not always

feel like doing what you know you should.

In Exodus 16 they came to the wilderness of Sin. Here their complaining resurfaced because of their lack of food. It was here that God instructed Moses about the manna that would fall daily (except for the Sabbath) to meet their provision.

The point of the bitter water in Marah and the lack of food in Sin were the need for patience in the lives of the people. God knew their need before they did. That is why He had already planted the tree in Marah years before. He knew in advance He would rain bread down from Heaven to meet their need in the wilderness. They needed to exercise patience, knowing He would supply their need as always.

The message is exactly the same today. Even as a tree was cut down and used to meet the need of bitterness in Marah, God used another tree at Calvary to meet our need. After tasting the bitterness of sin, we cast the tree of Calvary into our bitterness and God turns our bitterness into sweetness. We come to our "wilderness of Sin" and find no nourishment for our hungry soul; and then Heaven rains down the incarnate Son of God, the Lord Jesus Christ, who is the "bread of life" (John 6:48). We partake of Him and find that "if any man eat of this bread, he shall live for ever" (John 6:51).

Why is it that so many people are quitters? Because it's easy to quit! But if Marah and the wilderness of Sin teach us anything, they teach us this: Victory is just around the corner!

Why is it that so many people are quitters?

What else did Paul say we would have to be approved "in" as ministers of God? In "afflictions." I don't know about you, but I wish he hadn't said that! Afflictions are trials under pressure. Afflictions mean you are pressed down by circumstances. It suggests you are burdened and troubled. I have found that emotional troubles are more taxing than physical troubles. Often we can take a pill for the physical disorder, but emotional disorders are not easily cured.

The third thing Paul mentioned in this emotional war was "necessities." This refers to the everyday hardships of life. The hardship of paying the electric bill; the hardship of a flat tire; the hardship of so much to do and so little time to do it in. Life, in general, is often a pain.

"Distresses" were the last thing Paul mentioned as an emotional battlefield. Distresses are life's narrow places. It's those experiences that push us into a corner. Or, as the old cliché states, "You're between a rock and a hard place." But God delights in these times. As someone has so wisely stated, "When there's no way out, there's a way up!"

The second war we must wage is *physical.* 2 Corinthians 6:5 mentions three areas of physical conflict. The first is "in stripes." Paul was all too familiar with the cracking of the whip. Five times he was given thirty-nine lashes by the Jews and three times was beaten with rods. Once he was stoned at Lystra. I imagine Paul preached many a sermon with a black eye. He probably had to limp up to the pulpit. He may have talked slow and deliberate because his lip was swollen. Most of our churches wouldn't have Paul as their preacher because he was in more fights than an alley cat!

The second area of physical conflict for Paul was "in imprisonments." Paul's second home was a jail. Many times he received his "issued baloney sandwich" from the Roman guard. He had been an alley cat; now he is a jailbird! Can't you just see visitors to the church of Ephesus leaving the church never to return because the preacher had just been released from prison? I'm not sure our modern-day churches would have Paul as their pastor. The chairman of deacons would be most unnerved to announce to the Sunday morning congregation that we have a supply preacher today because Pastor Paul is in jail. I'm not sure a preacher like

Paul would be accepted in this day of contemporary church growth methods.

The third area of physical conflict was "in tumults." Tumults are riots. As I have studied my New Testament, I have found at least ten riots that broke out when Paul was in town. It may be that when we preach Jesus unashamedly a revival will break out. But it could be that, like Paul, a riot would break out! God allowed this man to write most of the New Testament; and next to Jesus, we consider him to be the greatest preacher/evangelist/missionary ever. Yet I find myself not bearing the testimony that this man did. I have often asked myself the question: How much of my life resembles first-century Christianity? Most of us lay down the banner over matters that would have been peanuts to Paul. The water doesn't have to be too bitter in Marah before we're ready to hang it up! What is the price of a great testimony? All you have. Nothing less will do. Paul bears the testimony of the old hymn, "I Surrender All":

All to Jesus I surrender,
All to him I freely give;
I will ever love and trust him,
In his presence daily live.
I surrender all,
I surrender all;
All to thee, my blessed Savior,
I surrender all.[1]

The third battle we must wage is *mental.* Paul mentions three areas of mental conflict in 2 Corinthians 6:5. The first is "in labors." This means hard work. It's no wonder so few have a good testimony. Someone once said, "Most Americans have quit working, but thank God they still have a job." I remember as a boy growing up that people would

What is the price of a great testimony?
All you have. Nothing less will do.

say of a lazy man: "A drop of his sweat is so precious it would cure cancer." I am grateful to have learned a work ethic in the tobacco fields of Lumberton, North Carolina: Hard work was more mental than physical! It was a discipline of the mind. Anyone can work for a little while, but it takes discipline to continue when you are tired.

It is a disgrace to God for a Christian to carry the testimony of laziness. The Bible clearly teaches us to work hard.

> "And whatsoever ye do, do it heartily, as to the Lord" (Colossians 3:23)

> "Whatsoever thy hand findeth to do, do it with thy might" (Ecclesiastes 9:10).

We're so afraid today that we will burn out when the vast majority is rusting out. I know a lot of people messing up, but I don't know very many burning out. The old statement is still true: "The world is moved by weary men." Kemin Wilson, founder of Holiday Inns, when asked how he became successful, replied, "I really don't know why I'm here. I never got a degree, and I've only worked half-days my entire life. I guess my advice is to do the same: Work half-days every day. And it doesn't matter which half: the first twelve hours or the second twelve hours."

I constantly remind my congregation that the average church member is under-challenged. We have sharp people in our pews desiring to be a part of something big, and we give them a job at the Kool-Aid stand. We say people won't attend a service over one hour, so we cut it down to fifty-five minutes. We have determined that Sunday nights are not convenient for people, so we eliminate the Sunday evening worship of God. I am concerned that we have built laziness and a lack of commitment into Christian people. It used to be asked of the old circuit-riding preachers, who pastored several churches, if they were going to slow down a little and they would reply, "What for? We've got all eternity to rest."

The second area of mental conflict is "in watchings." This means having a few sleepless nights. Not because the enchilada at dinner was too spicy but because the burdens and cares of the ministry were so severe. I must confess that I do not know of many Christians losing sleep over the things of God.

The third area of mental conflict is "in fastings." Many would think this conflict belongs under the heading of physical warfare, not mental. But if you've fasted much, you recognize the mental battle that takes place is far more brutal than the physical. Again, I must say I know too few Christians today who practice fasting for the purpose of focusing on God and His work.

This area of mental conflict is strongly attacked by Satan. The old devil knows if he can get you to think wrong then he can get you to feel wrong and do wrong. He would rather pollute your mind than pollute your body. The very reason

Lucifer brought physical infirmities upon Job was so he could get him to think different about God.

The greatest obstacle to the progression of the Gospel is the bad example of professing Christians. The unsaved use the inconsistencies of the saints as an excuse for rejecting Jesus Christ. Our testimony testifies to a hypocritical life. Know ing this, Paul said:

> "But I keep under my body, and bring it into subjection: lest that
> by any means, when I have preached to others, I myself should be
> a castaway" (1 Corinthians 9:27).

It has been my observation that most of us are too occupied with building our credentials than with building our testimony. It used to be that people would get involved in making a difference in people's lives. In the church they would teach Sunday School, go visiting, be responsible to fulfill their commitments, etc. Today many of our churches are full of uncommitted, unconcerned people. We used to call that person a hypocrite; today we call him busy!

It has been my observation that most of us
are too occupied with building our
credentials than with building our testimony.

When I came to pastor the First Baptist Church of Woodstock, Georgia, they had fired a preacher and a Minister of Music and the church had split. A pastor came and took me to lunch, welcomed me to the community, and advised me to preach and love the people but not to expect too much. He warned against believing that the church would grow; and therefore, I would be wise to settle in, not upset the status quo, and be a good, little ole pastor. Just one thing wrong with that: There's no such thing as a good little, ole Hell! And we've been entrusted with the message of "rescue the perishing, care for the dying."[2] God help us! We need to have the mental attitude that bears the testimony of a New Testament believer.

There's no such thing as a good little, ole Hell!

Let's say you so labor in the kingdom's work that you go to Heaven a little earlier. My question is: What's so bad about that? We sing: "When we all get to heaven what a day of rejoicing that will be."[3] We ought to live like we believe that or else quit singing it!

The Weapons He Used

You may think I am advocating spiritual suicide by waging the war for your testimony. However, there are spiritual weapons with which we can fight these battles. We need to understand that we are to go to war, but we must also understand how we are to go. If there is a testimony to be made, then we must use spiritual tools for our spiritual trials. Just as there is a war, there are weapons; just as there is resistance, there are resources.

The resources provided by God's amazing grace and the believer's attitude are more than a match for any difficulty. We must appropriate these by faith in God and His Word. Apart from these, life's difficulties will overwhelm us and the war for our testimony will be lost. These weapons are divine enablements and will equip us to go the distance. When we use them as our artillery, we will build a testimony that lasts.

In 2 Corinthians 6:4-5 Paul was "in" patience, afflictions, necessities, distresses, stripes, imprisonments, tumults, labors, watchings, and fastings. These describe the war that he was "in." But in 2 Corinthians 6:6, we see a prepositional change. Where Paul used the preposition "in," he now uses "by." Paul says he was "in" all these things, but he made it "by... ." Paul survived his warfare "by" nine weapons that he used to do battle. Three of these are *inward weapons*, and six are *outward weapons*.

The first of the *inward weapons* is "pureness." Pureness means to be clean morally and ethically. It describes one whose life is pure both in action and in attitude. It represents integrity in our motives, our methods, our means, and our message. Of all the spiritual weapons, purity is the most important one. If this is not a reality in your life, then the other eight weapons are rendered useless and inoperable.

Of all the spiritual weapons, purity is the most important one.

My life verse is Proverbs 20:7:

> "The just man walketh in his integrity: his children are blessed after him."

I carry a picture of my family in my Bible so that, as I travel, it will be a deterrent to temptation. I don't want to be a good Christian in the public eye and not be one first of all, at home. As I sit on the platform on Sunday mornings and look over my congregation, I realize that my victory does not come by being their pastor; my victory comes through pure living. The goal of my life is not to be a great preacher (although I want to be the best I can). My life's goal is to be a great Christian. You see, a person could be a great preacher and die and go to Hell. But you cannot be a great Christian and die and go to Hell. Therefore, the number one trait of the person winning the war for their testimony is purity.

> *A person could be a great preacher*
> *and die and go to Hell.*
> *But you cannot be a great Christian*
> *and die and go to Hell.*

The second *inward weapon* that we need to possess is "knowledge." Knowledge is a comprehension of God's truth and His ways. Knowledge comes through a diligent study of God's Word. This weapon is grossly neglected. It is neglected in a lot of churches. Sometimes our banquets are more important than our Bible studies and our socials more valued than our sermons. One thing we better nail down if we are to have a testimony that testifies: We cannot be a proper disciple apart from the Blessed Book! I hear some pseudo-church growth experts say that your doctrine is not important. May I say, it is most important! You are what you believe. If not, then the Bible is not true when it says, "As a man thinketh in his heart, so is he" (Proverbs 23:7). What you believe determines who you are and what you do. If you choose to detonate this weapon, you become highly vulnerable to lose the battle for your testimony.

The third *inward weapon* is "long-suffering" which is patience with difficult people. This empowers one to avoid retaliation when opposed. I recall hearing about a preacher who had this kind of long-suffering. He had a few disgruntled church members who wanted to run him off. One night they called a special church business meeting. At the meeting, the leader of the mutiny enumerated to the congregation all the reasons why the pastor should go. When he finished, he asked the pastor to come to the microphone and list the reasons why he should stay. The wise pastor came to the platform and said, "I refuse to list the reasons as to why I should stay. Because my friends don't need them and my enemies wouldn't believe them if they had them." He then sat down.

Paul continues his listing of our weaponry by recording six *outward weapons*. The first of which is "kindness." Kindness is something we all need to receive from others. I have learned that yesterday's kindness will only take you so far. We all need a good dose of kindness every day.

Weapons are used only in times of conflict. So it is with the weapon of kindness. It is needed in times of conflict. Anyone can be kind in the good times. But when the air is heavy with artillery fire, the weapon of kindness needs to be employed.

The second *outward weapon* is the "Holy Ghost." The Holy Spirit lives within every true believer and might be considered an inward weapon. However, the evidence of the Holy

Spirit ought to give testimony so others can see the super-natural power that resides within. Paul expounds on the outward display of a Spirit-filled life in Ephesians 5:18 - 6:9. He gives three qualifiers for the person who is "not drunk with wine, wherein is excess; but filled with the Spirit" (verse 18). A Spirit-filled person will...

1) Have a song in their heart (5:19).

2) Be thankful and grateful (5:20).

3) Be submissive (5:21-22; 6:1, 5).

The third *outward weapon* is "love unfeigned." This kind of love is genuine and contains no ulterior motive. Often we "love" because it's in our best interest to "love." This is not the kind of love that Paul is talking about. He's talking about a Jesus-kind of love. One that has the best interests of others at heart. One that represents *agape*-type love. When we per-sonify this kind of love, we have a most powerful weapon that will build a strong testimony. It really is true that people do not care how much you know until they first know how much you care.

The fourth *outward weapon* is "the word of truth." This is an absolute weapon for our arsenal because it is the message from God. This was the basis for Paul's ministry, his bold-ness and his security. We live in a time overrunning with knowledge but devoid of truth. So we ask, "What is truth?" Truth is a person; truth is Jesus Christ. Testifying of Himself, He said;

> "I am the way, the truth, and the life: no man cometh unto the Father, but by me" (John 14:6).

Truth isn't truth if it doesn't contain Jesus. We need to hold
the truth of His Word up to our face like a mirror to see if
we're reflecting the Son of God. When we live within the
word of truth, we can live as bold as an Apostle Paul. Truth
is not afraid of a challenge. It has nothing to hide and nothing to protect. Truth can and will stand on its own.

The fifth *outward weapon* is "the power of God." God's
power lifts the labor of our lives above mere human effort
with a divine energizing. If we are using the inward weapons
and the other outward weapons, then we will have the power
of God upon us. The word for "power" used here by Paul is
the Greek *dunamis*. It refers to a miraculous enablement.
We get our word *dynamite* from it. Paul used this word often.

> "Whereof I was made a minister, according to the gift of the grace
> of God given unto me by the effectual working of his power
> *(dunamis)"* (Ephesians 3:7).

> "Now unto him that is able to do exceeding abundantly above all
> that we ask or think, according to the power *(dunamis)* that wor-
> keth in us" (Ephesians 3:20).

The power of God upon our lives magnifies our efforts. God
takes our little ole feeble effort and places it under His mag-
nifying glass and it becomes more than we ever dreamed.

The sixth and last *outward weapon* is "the armor of righteousness." Proper armor prepares a soldier for battle. No
armor is worthy of spiritual battle if it is not righteous. This
"armor of righteousness" will equip the Christian for every
sort of struggle. It supplies the appropriate defensive and
offensive equipment necessary to win the war for your testimony. Again, Paul details this armor for us in Ephesians
6:10-17.

The Worthiness He Gained

Paul was viewed with much worth by those he led to the Lord Jesus and to whom he ministered the Word of God. However, the man of God is not so esteemed by the world. But the grace of God countered every false and ugly allegation with the glorious reality of a transformed life. Paul records nine "spiritual opposites" in 2 Corinthians 6:8-10 that were opinions of him:

- I am honored and dishonored.

- I have an evil report and a good report.

- I am considered a deceiver yet a truth-bearer.

- I am unknown yet well known.

- I am dying yet I live.

- I am punished but not put to death.

- I am sorrowful yet I always rejoice.

- I am poor yet have made many rich.

- I have nothing but possess all things.

Some had high opinions of Paul, others despised him; some gossiped about him, others supported him; some did not know him as a man of God, others knew he was a man of God; some were punishing him, while others were protecting him; some hated him, while others dearly loved him. One thing was for sure with Paul - he had a testimony! And his testimony was of more importance to him than his credentials. Can you imagine a church pulpit committee reviewing Paul's resume? As noted earlier in this chapter, he was an alley cat and a jailbird. If that would not upset the pulpit committee, then his references may have sealed his fate. Included in the list of people who knew Paul would have been an evil spirit. Acts 19:13-15 records the account:

> "Then certain of the vagabond Jews, exorcists, took upon them to call over them which had evil spirits the name of the Lord Jesus, saying, We adjure you by Jesus whom Paul preacheth. And there were seven sons of one Sceva, a Jew, and chief of the priests, which did so. And the evil spirit answered and said, Jesus I know, and Paul I know; but who are ye?"

Like Paul, the godly testimony you make will testify of your worthiness and impact generations to come.

Problems, Potential, Priorities

Life is full of problems. In fact, life is living from problem to problem and trying to make the best of it. Problems may be considered the greatest obstacle to a good testimony; but they also represent the greatest opportunity for a good testimony. The issue at stake is not problems brought on by the curse and consequence of our sin nature but the problem of sin in our lives. In this life we all will have great toil, great trouble and great tribulation. Why? Because sin operates in our world. This will ultimately culminate in all of us dying. However, the problem we must encounter to protect our testimony is that of unconfessed, unrepentant sin in our individual lives.

But life is also full of potential. God created us with so much to give. He has packed us full of energy, talents, enthusiasm, creativity, love, etc. Potential means we have an untapped resource of God's creativity within us. We need to activate that which our Father has endowed within us instead of allowing it to lie dormant. Jesus said, "It is more blessed to give than to receive" (Acts 20:35). By adhering to His command, we maximize our potential, help others and become more like God than ever before: "For God so loved the world that he *gave*..." (John 3:16). Therefore, He expects us to give of ourselves so that we can unleash and develop this potential.

Life is full of problems, full of potential but devoid of proper priorities. Priorities are simply the precedents you set for life. Priorities deal with how you arrange life. Those things that are significant to you are your priorities. Significant factors are established by your walk rather than your talk. When I properly prioritize my life, I lay a strong foundation for a good testimony.

Life becomes a continual mix of problems, potential and priorities:

- Personal problems may hinder our testimony.

- Personal potential can help our testimony.

- Personal priorities are the heart of our testimony.

Processing these is a lifelong endeavor which produces a beautiful testimony for the Lord Jesus if done correctly. There are six characteristics of the person who deals appropriately with their problems, potential and priorities: dignity, discipline, direction, diligence, decisiveness, and devotion.

Dignity

Dignity should be a priority for us; dignity is a God-given potential in us. Lack of dignity would be a problem for any of us. Dignity means to be held in high esteem and to be honored. It means you have a good reputation and are respected by others. This distinction does not come with a title or position but is earned day by day. And what is earned in a lifetime can be lost in minutes. Dignity has three constant companions: humility, integrity and purity. They travel life's journey with him to ever keep his way. Without them he would be lost and helpless, but together they make a powerful team.

> *This distinction does not come with a title or position but is earned day by day. And what is earned in a lifetime can be lost in minutes.*

The first such companion is humility.

> "...for God resisteth the proud, and giveth grace to the humble. Humble yourselves therefore under the mighty hand of God, that he may exalt you in due time." (1 Peter 5:5-6).

Modern psychology has taught us to be assertive and promote ourselves. We ought to exercise the gifts and talents that God has endowed us with; however, we must allow Him and others to bring honor and promotion to our lives. Proverbs 15:33 says that "before honor is humility." Therefore, when we pursue and assert humility in our lives, then others will insert honor.

The second companion is integrity which carries the idea of completeness and wholeness. Integrity characterizes the whole person as one of honesty and sincerity. And an honest, transparent soul is a haven for the Spirit of God. The American Management Association asked five thousand employees this question: "What values do you look for and admire in your superiors?" The top two answers were honesty and transparency.

Proverbs 10:9 says a person of integrity walks securely. To the person of integrity, fear and worry are strangers. Billy Graham has said he wants to be remembered as a man of integrity. As I stated in chapter two, my life verse is Proverb 20:7:

> "The just man walketh in his integrity: his children are blessed after him."

This is one of the greatest promises in the Word of God. We give our children cradles, clothes, cars and college; but the greatest inheritance we can bestow upon them is a mom and dad walking in integrity.

The third companion is purity which is clean, innocent, and gives a clear conscience. The old French proverb provided the best sleeping pill known when it instructed, "The softest pillow in the world is a clear conscience." Opposing this thought was Adolph Hitler who said, "I want to raise a generation devoid of conscience." Hitler was apparently devoid of conscience and wisdom, for wisdom knows that lack of conscience is a result of deficiency of purity. And a world stripped of purity would be reeling in a backward spiral. On the other hand, anyone clean and pure can move forward without the barrier of self-restraint and without the fear of innuendo.

"The softest pillow in the world is a clear conscience."

Nothing empowers me like being pure before the Lord God. Jerry Kirk said, "Purity, in its essence, is a reflection of God's character and presence in our lives." Jesus said in Matthew

5:8: "Blessed are the pure in heart: for they shall see God."
The implication of this verse, "for they shall see God," draws
our attention to a future time; but I believe it also has present implications upon our lives. In my humble opinion,
"the pure in heart" will see God in the here and now because
God moves in the lives of the pure-hearted.

These three companions are indispensable to dignity. They
all are interwoven throughout the Scripture as the Lord
describes and sets the standard for the person of dignity. As
C. K. Chesterson said, "Morality, like art, consists in drawing
a line somewhere. We must let God's Word draw the line, not
culture." But I am concerned that the culture keeps drawing
us further and further into immorality. We have become like
the frog placed into the pot of water. Ever so slowly, the heat
is applied and the water temperature increases until finally
the frog has been cooked for supper. Had the heat risen
immediately in the pot, the frog would have leaped from the
boiling water. But gradually he became adjusted and comfortable with his environment until he became a victim of it!

But gradually he became adjusted and comfortable with his environment until he became a victim of it!

You see, the real test of our testimony is not the big events
we're involved in but rather our faithfulness and obedience
in the little things of life. A person of dignity arms himself
with biblical principles and sacrifices anything that inter-
feres with his calling as a parent, spouse and Christian.

When a person loses his humility, integrity and purity, he loses his dignity which causes him to lose his testimony. Without dignity there is:

- No power
- No presence of God
- Oftentimes, no family
- Oftentimes, no future
- Oftentimes, no position
- No joy
- No respect
- No victory

The list reveals just how much we are willing to sacrifice on the altar of immorality! A major characteristic of a holy person is dignity. I'm of the deep conviction that a person of humility, integrity and purity will live a different, separated lifestyle. If you claim to be a Christian, then you don't go to the grocery store and fill your cart full of beer. There ought to be major, distinguishing characteristics of a Christian that link him inseparably with the working process of dignity in his life. There is a real problem with the person who flippantly talks about being a Christian and lives so unlike Jesus Christ!

This process of dignity is taught by the Apostle Peter to persecuted Christians.

> "Wherein ye greatly rejoice, though now for a season, if need be, ye are in heaviness through manifold temptations: That the trial of your faith, being much more precious than of gold that perisheth, though it be tried with fire, might be found unto praise and honor and glory at the appearing of Jesus Christ" (1 Peter 1:6-7).

We need God to periodically remove the alloys from our character. The eternal Goldsmith turns up the heat, melts the gold to liquid form and then scrapes the impurities from the surface. Likewise, the heat of life brings the alloys from within the precious metal of the human soul to the surface so that they can be removed. It is evident that we all have impurities within. But this extracting is a process that God does over and over again. Why? To continually purify us for His honor and glory and to keep us from becoming over-whelmed and discouraged. If He brought all of them to the surface at once, we would lose heart. So He cools the pot down and reheats it again at a later time.

I once heard of a man who came down during the invitation each night of a week long revival. Each night he confessed a different sin because God was reheating the pot in his life to draw out the impurities. At the conclusion of the revival ser-vices, someone confronted him about going to the altar every night of the revival and asked why he did that. The newly cleansed man replied, "Because I didn't want to be like you!"

Discipline
So many blame others or circumstances when they do not reach their potential by claiming how they have tried to live godly. But godly living is not an event to participate in or a seminar to attend; it is a process. As the ancient saying goes, "A journey of a thousand miles begins with the first step." Dignity is an ongoing process - much like moral failure which is rarely the result of a blowout but almost always due to a slow leak. The Bible refers to us *backsliding,* not *back-falling.* Usually, we do not take a plunge into gross sin. It is

the result of a slow leak in our character and our habits. We "slide" away from God little by little until we are far removed from Him. The daily disciplines ignored in our lives provide Satan, the roaring lion, with easy prey.

> ## *Usually, we do not take a plunge into gross sin. It is the result of a slow leak in our character and our habits.*

A lack of discipline will create many problems. An abundance of discipline will project you to the height of your potential. But it all boils down to disciplining yourself in the area of your priorities. I want to suggest three areas where discipline cannot be neglected if we are to keep our testimony intact.

The first area is our private life. This area of your life is where no one goes but you and God. Your spouse is not even allowed there. This area is the deep recess of your soul; this area is where the "slow leaks" begin. Two compartments of this area are your thought life and your devotional life.

No one knows your thoughts but you and God. I love Matthew's two records of Christ's knowledge of people's thoughts:

> "And Jesus knowing their thoughts said, Wherefore think ye evil in your hearts?" (9:4).

> "And Jesus knew their thoughts, and said unto them..." (12:25).

I am amazed at how we think we can avoid God's knowledge of our thoughts - like Adam and Eve did after their sin. Let's get one thing straight: God knows our every thought!

Why are our thoughts so important? Proverbs 23:7 says, "For as he thinketh in his heart, so is he..." Your private thought life is what reproduces itself in the other areas of life. We must understand that we are no better publicly than we have been privately. This is why we must have an active devotional life. By spending time with God in His Word and through prayer, we develop and adopt His thoughts and are thus "conformed to the image of his Son" (Romans 8:29). There are basically two ways you get to know someone: by spending time with the person or reading about the person. Bible study and prayer give us both.

> ## *We must understand that we are no better publicly than we have been privately.*

Each day I give the first forty-five minutes to be with the Lord. I spend time reading the Word and praying. For several years I have made reading the Proverbs part of my time in the Bible. I read the chapter that corresponds to the day of the month so that each month I read though the entire book of Proverbs. I read other passages as well, but I have found I need the wisdom that Proverbs offers to conduct my life appropriately. Another practical thing I have done is to designate a special place that has become my haven, my sanctuary for my devotional time. It is here that I spend time loving and worshiping God at the start of each new day that He gives me. I once heard Dr. Adrian Rogers, Pastor of the great Bellevue Baptist Church in Memphis, Tennessee, say we do not go to church to worship; we bring our worship to church. This may explain why our churches are so dead and devoid of true worship.

I do know that Satan fights nothing harder than my quiet time with God each day. I have found that the enemy attacks my spiritual defenses. It reminds me of the news that I watched during the short war with Iraq. The media reported the areas where the enemy had military buildups and how our troops would attack these strongholds. If we are smart enough to do this, you know Satan is. Therefore, we need to take time to be holy. Or, as the psalmist said, "Be still, and know that I am God..." (Psalm 46:10).

The second area where discipline must be exercised is in our personal life. A small circle of family members and friends shares this area of your life. Disciplines here expose your attitudes more than any other area. We all have the tendency to be who we really are around those who are closely related to us. Therefore, guard your attitude so that you produce the fragrance of Christ as you interact with these loved ones.

In a practical way, let me share some disciplines I try to perform. I want my wife and two daughters to know me as a man of God at home more than at church. I never want one of my daughters to hear someone compliment me only to think: "Boy, if you could only see him rant and rave at home!" Being a Christian at the supper table is more valuable to me than being a Christian in the pulpit. I want my family to know that what I am preaching is real and alive in my heart. I'm not near as interested in what the deacons think of my sermons as I am my wife and girls. The criticisms of others

can be endured as long as those closest to me know that I am
a man of God. The greatest testimony you can possess is to
have those who know you best to love and respect you most.

The greatest testimony you can possess is to have those who know you best to love and respect you most.

I work real hard at maintaining time with my family. I have
adopted the following formula to spend time with my wife
Janet:

• Dialogue daily

It doesn't matter where I am - I always try to call my wife
every day to talk with her. I occasionally must compromise
this when I am out of the country, but I make no other
allowances in violating this rule.

• Date weekly

Once a week we enjoy going out to dinner, taking in a movie
or going to the racetrack where I serve as "Racetrack
Chaplain."

• Depart quarterly

We enjoy getting away to refocus and "clear the cobwebs out
of our minds." It is a great time for us to spend quality time
with each other without any disturbances. I have discovered
that I must take time to be holy, but I also must take time to
be hubby.

I also have prioritized time with my two girls. Both Deanna and Hollie are grown and married. But when they were still at home, I would take them with me on trips and speaking engagements. I wanted to hang out with them, and I also desired for them to be present when the glory of God fell. If I was speaking at a conference with other pastors or Bible teachers, they would get to meet and hear many great men of God. I wanted to build in them a respect for those who were giants in the faith. I also have "dated" my daughters by taking them out to nice restaurants, going shopping with them, etc. I wanted them to know they are important to their dad. When people are dying, I often hear the regretful words; "I spent too much time at the office." I never heard a dying person say, "I spent too much time with my family." Don't let your greatest regret be that which you cherish the most. The most cherished thing in life is not possessions but relationships! When you break life down to its lowest denominator, all you have is relationships. When the money, possessions and prestige are gone, all you have left are the memories, friendships and associations with others.

I never heard a dying person say, "I spent too much time with my family."

The third area of discipline is our professional life. It is easy to become so task-oriented and purpose-driven that we run over people to accomplish our "Mission Statement." If your purpose in life cannot be accomplished without destroying other people, then you are not following God's purpose for your life. Christians are in the people business. Therefore, we should constantly be touching people, reaching out to people and ministering to people. We should enhance people's lives like Jesus did. Everywhere He went, He was touching, reaching and ministering to people. Like Jesus, we need to be aware of our call to be in the "people business." I want to remember this when I'm at the restaurant and my steak is not prepared exactly as I desired. I want to remember this when I pick my clothes up at the cleaners. I want to remember this when I take my car to the car wash. Everywhere we go, we are "ambassadors for Christ" (2 Corinthians 5:20). We're not representing just anyone; we represent the King of Kings and the Lord of Lords! This is why Jesus taught us to "love thy neighbor as thyself" (Matthew 22:39). It seems the Golden Rule has become tarnished in this day of success at any cost.

Evangelist Junior Hill once told a group of pastors: "If you're too big for the little churches, then you're too little for the big churches." I want to say the same applies to our relationships: If we're too big for the little guy, then we're too little for the big guy. If you don't have time for people, then they will not take time for you. Dr. Jerry Falwell was preaching at our church and shared the following five rules of life:

- No quick fixes
- No real bargains
- No permanent solutions (except salvation)
- Very few repeats
- Not many "forever" friends

A man came into my office one day and said, "Normally, when an influential person does wrong, he loses those who are close around him." Then he began to weep and said, "I don't care what you do. I'll always be your friend." He made an allegiance to me that day to be a "forever" friend. Has it impacted me? You bet it has. Seven years have past, and I still remember it.

Remember, Mr. Professional, you need people. Not as instruments to use to propel you to the top but as valuable contributors to help make you a whole person. As Proverbs 27:17 admonishes: "Iron sharpeneth iron; so a man sharpeneth the countenance of his friend." In the ministry, we are not in the business of building the church as much as we are building people. Paul instructed in Ephesians 4:12 that we are to equip the saints for the work of the ministry. If we would spend more time building up people and less time building the church, then we would see the church grow!

Therefore, keep these three things in mind:

- You can't treat people wrongly and please God.

- Treat everyone you meet like you want to be treated.

- The people you interact with are the same people for whom God gave His Son. The Father greatly loves them!

Direction

The direction of our life reveals our true priorities. Someone once said, "Show me your calendar and your checkbook, and I will show you your priorities." Where you spend your money and your time exposes your true priorities. Priorities are so important because I'm finding that most people have few of them. Let me give you some helps in establishing your priorities.

First of all, have a clear vision of where you are going and communicate it regularly. I oftentimes remind our staff to plan with the end in mind. In other words, when all is said and done, be where you wanted to be. If you don't know where you're headed with the project, then don't start it. The Bible says that without vision the people perish. (Proverbs 29:18) We need to retreat from the busyness of life and reflect on the following questions:

- Where is my life going?

- If it continues as is, what will it look like in ten years? Twenty years?

- Am I doing what I really love?

- If I could do only one thing in life, what would it be?

- Do I really know what I want out of life?

Secondly, talk your vision over with your spouse or your closest friend. This will make for some great conversation. Your spouse or intimate friend can make tremendous contributions to your dream. When you partner-up, your strength increases many times over. Ecclesiastes 4:9-12 states it best:

> "Two are better than one; because they have a good reward for their labor. For if they fall, the one will lift up his fellow: but woe to him that is alone when he falleth; for he hath not another to help him up. Again, if two lie together, then they have heat: but how can one be warm alone? And if one prevail against him, two shall withstand him; and a threefold cord is not quickly broken."

Thirdly, spend less time managing others and more time leading. Many people try to manage others, but this cannot be done. You manage yourself; you lead others. When you manage yourself, you earn the right to lead others.

How do you lead others? By example. Jesus was the Master
Teacher, yet His greatest teaching was through His living.

Fourthly, know what is important to you and do it. So many
do the things that are not really important and have no significant value or contribution. We Americans are so busy
with "stuff" that we don't have time for the significant. We
are involved in a whirlwind of activity but void of accomplishment. This is also true of the church. We have bake
sales, garage sales, banquets, parties, multitudes of commit-
tees and meetings, fundraisers...whew! I'm getting tired
thinking about it. However, are these activities accomplish-
ing something? As one sage put it: "When all is said and
done, more is said than done!" Find that which is important;
cut out the "busy stuff"; and focus on the things that produce.

Hebrews 12:1-2 exhorts us:

> "...let us lay aside every weight, and the sin which doth so easily
> beset us, and let us run with patience the race that is set before us,
> Looking unto Jesus the author and finisher of our faith..."

These two verses teach us three things about running a race:

  • Runners free themselves of extra clothing, gear, etc.

Runners cannot encumber themselves by unnecessary
clothing and gear. They must be unrestricted and free so all
their energies are focused on one goal - winning the race.

  • Runners stay in their designated lane.

They do not run in several lanes. They know their own lane
and stay in it. Like runners, God has equipped us and called
us to run in our lane. The more lanes we try to occupy, the

less likely we are to win the race.

• Runners focus on the finish line.

Runners do not look at their feet or their opponent. They look straight ahead to the goal. If you focus on other things beside the finish line, you will never win the race!

Diligence

We need to be responsible and faithful. We have convinced ourselves that only the talented, gifted, and charismatic can be successful. However, I talk with many businessmen who are dying for responsible employees: those who will be at work on time; those who will give eight hours of work for eight hours of pay; those who will perform their job with diligence and excellence. In essence, employers and managers are desirous of responsible people in their companies. Winston Churchill said, "The price of greatness is responsibility."

"The price of greatness is responsibility."

The Apostle Paul was particularly appreciative of those who were diligent in their pursuits. Being the passionate, fiery man that he was, not many could measure up to the faithfulness that he embraced. But under Roman guard and confinement for two years, he wrote the four epistles of Ephesians, Philippians, Colossians and Philemon. In Colossians 4, he mentions eight men who were faithful, responsible, diligent servants of God. His testimony of these men stands 2,000 years later for us to read. Let's take notice of these men:

"All my state shall **Tychicus** declare unto you, who is a beloved brother, and a faithful minister and fellow servant in the Lord: Whom I have sent unto you for the same purpose,.that he might know your estate, and comfort your hearts." (vs. 7-8)

"With **Onesimus,** a faithful and beloved brother..." (v. 9)

"**Aristarchus** my fellow prisoner saluteth you..." (v. 10)

"...and **Marcus**..." (v. 10)

"And **Jesus**, which is called Justus..." (v. 11)

"**Epaphras**, who is one of you, a servant of Christ, saluteth you, always laboring fervently for you in prayers, that ye may stand perfect and complete in all the will of God. For I bear him record, that he hath a great zeal for you..." (vs. 12-13)

"**Luke**, the beloved physician..." (v. 14)

"...and **Demas**, greet you." (v. 14) (emphasis mine)

The first thing you notice about these men (beside the fact we can't pronounce most of their names) is their diligence in faithfully pursuing the call of God upon their lives. These men were far removed from family and comfortable surroundings. They had endangered their own lives and well-being for the sake of spreading the Gospel and uplifting the saints. O, how we need more Christians like this in our churches today! People who can be counted on; people who are not afraid to take a bold stand for the Good News; people who will be a servant of the Most High God; people who will find their place of service and stick to it! O, to God that our churches were known for people of this caliber! What a testimony we would have as individual Christians and as local churches.

Paul said of these men:

"These only are my fellow workers unto the kingdom of God, which have been a comfort unto me" (v. 11).

What a testimony these men bore by possibly the greatest Christian who ever lived. Of the thousands of Christians, Paul had only eight men by his side during this two-year period.

Vince Lombardi, the great coach of the Green Bay Packers known for spotting and producing winners, once said, "The quality of a person's life is in direct proportion to their commitment to excellence, regardless of their chosen field of endeavor." Bottom line: Be responsible, be faithful, be diligent!

Decisiveness

It seems to me that most Americans have a hard time making decisions. People's lives are in deadlock because they fear the ramifications of their decision. Now I don't want to encourage hasty, ill-advised decision-making; but neither do I want to see people so gripped by fear that they will not move forward. Someone once said the best thing you can do is make the right decision; the second best thing you can do is make the wrong decision; and the worst thing you can do is make no decision. Why? Because if you don't make a decision, then life will make one for you and it probably won't be God's best.

If you don't make a decision, then life will make one for you and it probably won't be God's best.

Let me illustrate. I hear these so-called church growth gurus say that people will not come to church for more than one hour on Sunday morning. Therefore, they suggest we cut our worship services down to fifty-five minutes and replace Sunday School with home cell groups during the week. However, I believe people will come and stay if we are committed to worshiping God, studying His Word and ministering to each other. The question is not: Will they stay? The question is: Will we be committed to the calling of God?

Recently, I attended a conference where a "church growth expert" said that people under thirty-five years of age would not attend church. So the following Sunday I asked all those under thirty-five to stand and the house was full of them. I'm sure many accepted this "expert" advice and modified their ministry based on this information. But have we stopped to decide for ourselves? Have we meditated on God's Word to discover what the Lord has to say about the issue?

You see, we have relegated ourselves to making the *safe* decisions instead of *surrendered* decisions. Don't go through life allowing others to make decisions for you. Allow yourself to be shoved out of your comfort zone and to live on the edge. It is then that you must depend on God to come through. Most of us, however, never place ourselves in a position to need God. We go along with the rest of the world and, thus, fall into the snare of the uncommitted and the unmoved! Elijah saw this in his day.

> "Elijah went before the people and said, *'How long will you waver between two opinions? If the* LORD *is God, follow him: but if Baal is God, follow him.'* But the people said nothing" (1 Kings 18:21 NIV, emphasis mine).

We go along with the rest of the world and, thus, fall into the snare of the uncommitted and the unmoved!

We are so afraid of potential dangers that we miss the adventure. There are three attitudes that surface in each of us as we approach life. They are seen in the following people:

- Caretakers - They have the *burden* of maintaining the status quo.

- Undertakers - They have the responsibility of *burying* the dead.

- Risktakers - They have the *blessing* of new adventures.

Devotion

Have you ever stopped to ask yourself this question: What am I really devoted to? The Bible answers this question for us in Matthew 22:36-40:

> "Master, which is the great commandment in the law? Jesus said unto him, Thou shalt love the Lord thy God with all thy heart, and with all thy soul, and with all thy mind. This is the first and great commandment. And the second is like unto it, Thou shalt love thy neighbor as thyself. On these two commandments hang all the law and the prophets."

Jesus taught that our devotion should be first to God, then to others. The Apostle John expanded this to say that a man who loves God will love others:

> "We love him, because he first loved us. If a man say, I love God, and hateth his brother, he is a liar: for he that loveth not his brother whom he hath seen, how can he love God whom he hath not

seen? And this commandment have we from him, That he who
loveth God love his brother also" (1 John 4:19-21).

Our love for God is made evident in the way we love others.
And if we love others, we will believe in them, give ourselves
to them, build relationships with them and trust them. A
Carnegie Foundation study, designed to determine what
contributes most to a person's success, found that 15% of a
person's success is determined by job knowledge and technical skills. Attitude and the ability to relate to others determine the other 85%.

Peter Blanchard, one of the foremost business writers,
encourages business leaders to take five steps in working
with their people:

- Tell them what to do.
- Show them what to do.
- Let them try.
- Observe their performance.
- Praise their progress.

We need to be devoted to those God has placed around us.
We should give them more than they expect and do so cheerfully because one is never more at his best than when he is
helping others. You see, the only way you ultimately win in
life is when you help others to win.

Are you devoted to others? Jesus was. Therefore, others
should be our priority. Philippians 2:3-5 says:

> "Let nothing be done through strife or vainglory; but in lowliness
> of mind let each esteem other better than themselves. Look not
> every man on his own things, but every man also on the things of
> others. Let this mind be in you, which was also in Christ Jesus."

*We should give them more than
they expect and do so cheerfully
because one is never more at his
best than when he is helping others.*

Problems: life is full of them.

Potential: life is full of it.

Priorities: life is determined by them!

Beavers, Fallen Trees, and Dammed-Up Lives

"In the last day, that great day of the feast, Jesus stood and cried saying, If any man thirst, let him come unto me, and drink. He that believeth on me, as the scripture hath said, out of his belly shall flow rivers of living water. (But this spake he of the Spirit, which they that believe on him should receive: for the Holy Ghost was not yet given; because that Jesus was not yet glorified" (John 7:37-39).

A friend of mine owns a large section of land with a beautiful river running through it. The soil along the river is rich and fertile because of the flow of the water. One day my friend began to notice that the river did not flow as it had before and that the plant life was beginning to dry up and die out. As he walked back upstream, he noticed some beavers had dammed up the river and restricted the flow of the life-giving waters. It was apparent the beavers had been working for some time, gathering fallen trees and constructing their dam.

As I pondered his situation, it became obvious to me that in this world we have beavers, fallen trees and dammed-up lives. The flow of living water has been stopped. The riverbeds of our lives no longer ooze with the swift running stream of God's Spirit. This story graphically illustrates the steps in our lives which eventually progress until we experience dryness in our spiritual vitality.

Step One: Beavers

We have beavers in our world today that can dam up our lives. What are these beavers? The adversary and his demons. Satan and his army of fallen angels not only want to dam up your life so that it becomes unproductive, but they desire to damn you eternally. His beavers work tirelessly, gathering the fallen trees. The Scripture admonishes us:

> "Be sober, be vigilant; because your adversary the devil, as a roaring lion, walketh about, seeking whom he may devour" (1 Peter 5:8).

Here are three observations about Satan from this passage:

1. He is *aggressive*. He is not just a lion; he is a *roaring* lion which indicates he is on the prowl. Satan is always roaring because he stays hungry and is never satisfied. He has destroyed millions of lives but still wants more.

2. He is *active*. We all need to realize that Satan is an eager beaver. He is walking about "seeking whom he may devour." In the first chapter of Job, he comes to the throneroom of God and the Lord asks him, "Whence comest thou?" And Satan answers, "From going to and fro in the earth, and from walking up and down in it" (Job 1:7). Make no mistake: Satan is active, and he is on the prowl. It also is worth noting that he was aware of Job and knew who he was. God asked him if he had considered Job and his uprightness. Satan not only knew him but even had his own explanation as to why he was so godly:

"Doth Job fear God for nought? Hast not thou made an hedge
about him, and about his house, and about all that he hath on
every side? thou hast blessed the work of his hands, and his substance is increased in the land" (Job 1:9-10).

Satan also had been analyzing the areas where Job might be
vulnerable: "But put forth thine hand now, and touch all that
he hath, and he will curse thee to thy face" (Job 1:11). Satan
is evil, a liar and a murderer; but lazy he is not.

3. He *annihilates.* He is a devourer who is playing for keeps.
He is pictured in the parable of the sower (Luke 8:5, 12) as
the one who devours the good seed of the Word of God that
falls upon our hearts. Satan, as a lion, consumes his prey.
We need to realize he is in the business of destroying lives.
However, God runs a construction business; He is building
lives. The devil is in the destruction business; he is wrecking
lives.

Step Two: Fallen Trees
Even as beavers use fallen, rotten trees to dam up a river,
satanic beavers use the debris and litter in our lives to
obstruct the flow of living water. Four types of fallen trees in
our lives are most useful to these evil beavers:

1. *Areas of weakness.* Even as Satan knew about Job, he
knows about you and me. He knows those areas in our lives
which are most vulnerable. It may be in the area of sex,
money, power, strong drink, etc.; but rest assured, Satan will
find that area and exploit it. Later in this chapter, we will dis-
cuss how to handle these areas so as not to give Satan a
cracked door to kick open in your life.

2. *Aimless intentions.* Beavers have an advantage over us in

that they work intentionally and purposefully. Conversely, most of us live with no real direction in life; we wander through our days aimlessly. Observation has taught me that most people's lives consist of going to work, paying bills and living it up on the weekends - only to do it all over again the next week. Is life not more than this? Did God place us here only with that purpose in mind? Granted, we all need to work and pay our bills - that is biblical. We also need some times of recreation and relaxation. But do we ever stop to ask: "For what purpose did God create me?"

But do we ever stop to ask: "For what purpose did God create me?"

I am reminded of a man who was speaking at a state mental hospital. Upon being introduced he stepped to the podium and asked, "Why are we all here?" In response one of the residents stood to his feet and replied, "Because we're not all here!" I am of the impression that most of us are not all here! We gleefully travel down life's road only to find that it is a cul-de-sac.

Like the beavers, we need to live intentionally and purposefully. We should set our goals to be good parents, live in subjection to the law, be honest, love our neighbors as ourselves, love the Lord with all our hearts, go to church every Lord's day, influence people's lives for good and allow Christ to live and love through us.

3. *Alignment with the world.* There seem to be more and

more of these fallen trees. Corruption has not been introduced to today's modern society by revolution but by dilution. Our morals and values have slowly been diluted by worldliness. Christians have become so aligned with the world that we have lost the ability to determine good and evil. Right and wrong are no longer what they used to be in our limited discernment.

Joshua 9 reveals how Joshua and the children of Israel made a pact with the Gibeonites. They were inhabitants in the Promised Land that God had just given to the Israelites. Although God had instructed the Jews to destroy the people of the land, they were deceived by the Gibeonites and made a covenant with them. Verse fourteen makes a profound statement concerning the lack of discernment on the part of Joshua and his leaders: "And the men [Israelites] took of their [Gibeonites'] victuals, and asked not counsel at the mouth of the Lord."

This indictment is true of believers today. We have accepted the counsel of the world and never stopped to ask: What does God say about this? When God speaks, it doesn't matter what anyone else has to say about the subject. Truth is not based upon consensus, opinions or modern culture; truth is dependent upon God. Jesus said, "I am the way, the truth, and the life..." (John 14:6). If we would only pause long enough to ask counsel of God and His Word, it would keep us from an unhealthy alignment with the world. How can we be clean from worldliness? Jesus answers that in John 15:3: "Now ye are clean through the word which I have spoken unto you."

Truth is not based upon consensus, opinions or modern culture; truth is dependent upon God.

4. *Acceptance of evil.* We have been so infiltrated with world-liness that we have actually accepted evil. Christians today hear things, read things and watch things that a few years ago would have produced an outcry! But today we bring it into our living rooms, give it to our kids and even boast of it to our friends. We have become a nation that tolerates sin. The prophet Isaiah warned of this:

> "Woe unto them that call evil good, and good evil; that put dark-ness for light, and light for darkness; that put bitter for sweet, and sweet for bitter!" (Isaiah 5:20).

We need to learn this principle: *The more accessible we are to sin, the more acceptable we are to sin.* Our society is a living testimony to this principle. This is why the Scriptures admonish us to "...resist the devil, and he will flee from you" (James 4:7). Peter, speaking of Satan as a roaring lion, says, "Whom resist steadfast in the faith" (1 Peter 5:9); and Paul, writing to the church at Ephesus, instructs, "Neither give place to the devil" (Ephesians 4:27). We are in gross error when we think we can flirt with sin; by so doing we expose ourselves to the devil. *That which we tolerate is that which we perpetuate.*

Step Three: Dammed-Up Lives
In step two the river's flow begins to be restricted. At this third stage, it is almost non-existent. The river is now a trick-le of water!

Oh, how our unguarded lives are so often dammed up by a bunch of beavers on the demonic *destruction* crew. Foreman Satan knows he cannot damn the Christian's soul, but he can restrict the Christian's flow. His workers toil until the riverbed that once overflowed the banks is now dry and parched. Over a period of time, they steal our vigor for

That which we tolerate is that which we perpetuate.

God. No longer is a fresh word of testimony found on our lips; no longer are we stirred with a passion for the Word of God; no longer are we interested in lost people who are dying without Jesus; no longer are we consumed with the moving of the Holy Spirit in our lives. Statistics reveal that most churches have less than fifty percent of their membership present on any given Sunday, a mere twenty percent tithe and only one out of fifty win anyone to faith in Christ in a year's time. What's gone wrong? Beavers, fallen trees and dammed-up lives!

Dynamite!

I asked my land-owning friend how he removed the dam to allow the river to flow once again. His reply: "Dynamite!" "I took four sticks of dynamite, wedged them into different sections of the dam, stepped back into the woods and blasted the dam away."

As I reflected upon this, I recalled that the original New Testament Greek word translated in the King James as "power" was *dunamis* (we studied this word in chapter two). For example, 1 Corinthians 1:24 calls Christ the "*dunamis* of

God." Even as the dam needed dynamiting to restore the flowing waters to the dry riverbed, so we need to plug our lives full of Jesus to eliminate the dam and restore the flow of living water to our dried-up souls. Ephesians 1:19-20 instructs us of God's mighty *dunamis:*

> "And what is the exceeding greatness of his power (dunamis) to us-ward who believe, according to the working of his mighty power, Which he wrought in Christ, when he raised him from the dead, and set him at his own right hand in the heavenly places."

Satan may have thought he had won the victory when Jesus was crucified; but God, by His mighty power, raised Jesus to victory.

This same power is available for each born-again, blood-bought Christian. Not only can Jesus *destroy* the work of Satan by His mighty power, but also He can *restore* the work of God by the same power.

How do we go about getting this *dunamis?* There are four simple, clear steps to relieve our lives of fallen trees:

1. *The Confession of Sin.* First John 1:9 says, "If we confess our sins, he is faithful and just to forgive us our sins, and to cleanse us from all unrighteousness." To confess our sins means to *agree* with God about our sin. God is truth. The Bible says Jesus is "full of grace and truth" (John 1:14). God does not simply know truth or adhere to truth: He *is* truth, and He says that we have all sinned. Romans 3:10 reads, "There is none righteous, no, not one." First John 1:10 provides strong support for this verse by saying, "If we say that we have not sinned, we make him a liar, and his word is not in us." The truth is: God is truth. So for us to agree with God

simply means we adhere to His truth about us.

To agree with God means we must change our way of thinking and adopt His way of thinking. Adrian Rogers once said, "The devil had rather get you to *think* wrong than to do wrong." You see, if you *do* wrong, you can confess it and God will forgive you. But if you think wrong about what you did wrong, you don't think anything is wrong! At this point you have become more *accessible* to sin and, therefore, more *acceptable* of sin.

> ## *If you think wrong about what you did wrong, you don't think anything is wrong!*

Our nation has become a sad testimony to this truth. There was a day in which we thought right about what was wrong; today we think wrong about what is right. Therefore, we can no longer differentiate between good and evil.

Our acceptable way of thinking has brought sin into the White House. Our government sanctions the murder of millions of unborn babies and appoints homosexuals and lesbians to top leadership positions - all in the name of fairness. In our government's attempt to give people their rights, we have facilitated their wrong.

Our acceptable way of thinking has brought sin into the courthouse. In our attempt to give criminals their rights, we have given society many wrongs.

Our acceptable way of thinking has brought sin into the

schoolhouse. In our attempt to teach what is right about our origins, we have taught what is wrong about our creation.

Our acceptable way of thinking has brought sin into the church house. In our attempt to treat people "right," we have wronged them by failing to tell them to repent. When we preachers of the Gospel fail to tell them what is right, we allow them to live that which is wrong. We are, in essence, giving people permission to neglect the Word of God and reject the Spirit of God. This, my friend, is wrong!

Our acceptable way of thinking has brought sin into your house. The place ordained by God as a haven for love has been wronged by violence, divorce, child abuse and incest.

Acceptable thinking replaces conviction with compromise, which leads to corruption. My friend, evangelist Bailey Smith states, "Any sin we cover, God uncovers." Adam and Eve attempted to cover their sin and nakedness with fig leaves; however, God came in the cool of the evening and uncovered their sin. Like our first parents, we are not in agreement with God when we accept and conceal our sin.

"Any sin we cover, God uncovers."

Jesus is not only full of truth; He is full of grace. The Greek word for "full" is *pleres* which conveys the meaning of being covered over. We could interpret this phrase by saying that Jesus was so full of grace and truth that He could hold no more. I rejoice that our Savior is so full of truth that He will tell me of my pitiful plight and my need to turn to Him, but I am equally delighted that He is full of grace and, therefore, will receive me. It should be the desire of each Christian to emulate Jesus and be full of grace and truth; the world so desperately needs both. But it also should be the longing of each local church to be full of grace and truth. When these two traits characterize our churches, then we will see more people coming to a saving knowledge of Jesus Christ.

To confess our sin also means to *acknowledge* our sin. Bailey further states, "Any sin we uncover, God covers." In order to uncover our sin, we must acknowledge that sin before a holy God.

"Any sin we uncover, God covers."

In Luke 18 Jesus told the parable about the prayers of a Pharisee and a publican. The Pharisee thanked God that he was not like the publican. However, the publican smote his breast and asked God to be merciful to him because he was a sinner. This parable poignantly expresses the difference between covering and uncovering your sin when Jesus, referring to the publican, said, "I tell you, this man went down to his house justified rather than the other..." (v. 14). The covering of sin brings grief to the soul; the uncovering of sin brings grace to the soul. The difference between the Pharisee and the publican had nothing to do with goodness, intellect or successfulness. The difference was all wrapped up in agreement and acknowledgement.

2. The Cleansing of Sin. God desires to remove our sin "as far as the east is from the west..." (Psalm 103:12). David cried out to God, "Create in me a clean heart, O God..." (Psalm 53:10). This is the very thing that God wants to do in our lives. Only as we receive the cleansing of God can we live fruitful, productive lives.

When we get saved, it is as if God gives our souls a good bath. He cleanses us from the inside out. This inward cleansing will become evident then in outward living. Before Christ our fruit is evil and defiled; after Christ our fruit is good and delicious. Cleansing brings communion with God, and we enjoy His friendship; it brings companionship with God, and we enjoy His fellowship.

Cleansing is not experienced by many because they are not willing to forsake their sin. I once dealt with a man living in adultery. He acknowledged his sin but refused to forsake it. He discussed his sin problem with me but was unwilling to turn from it. I could not help him; but by his refusal to turn from his wrong, even God couldn't help him. He could not bring himself to let go. On one hand, he wanted his wife. On the other hand, he desired to cling to his extramarital affair. Ultimately, he will lose one or the other. So it is with God. We cannot continue to have flowing rivers of living water with fallen trees in our lives. Eventually, we will lose one or the other.

I have the opportunity to speak at many men's conferences, and I constantly remind them that if they choose to live in sin they will get caught. Sin always baits its catch. Another great principle for us to learn is: *In life we must forsake certain things in order to possess others.*

3. *The Change from Sin.* On January 7, 1973, I received Jesus Christ as my personal Lord and Savior. Since that time I have never been the same. Jesus said, "If the Son therefore shall make you free, ye shall be free indeed" (John 8:36). I believe that when we are free *indeed* we will be free *in deed.* Jesus

sets you free, releases you from sin and empowers you to embark on a new and better way of living. When He comes into your heart, He gives you new direction by giving your life an about-face. You will no longer desire to walk the path that you have trod before because He changes you and gives you a new set of want-to's.

I believe that when we are free indeed we will be free in deed.

4. *The Control over Sin.* Jesus said in John 7:37, "If any man thirst, let him come unto me, and drink." What will happen then? "...out of his belly shall flow rivers of living water" (John 7:38). If you want to be filled with the Spirit so that you possess this outpouring of living water, then thirst for Jesus and drink of Him continually! Jesus also said, "...Except ye eat the flesh of the Son of man, and drink his blood, ye have *no* life in you" (John 6:53). Without Jesus one cannot possess the river of flowing water because he is all dammed up.

I asked my friend one final question: "What took place when the dynamite exploded?" His answer: "The waters began flowing once again and they carried all the fallen trees and debris downstream." So it is with our lives. When we partake of Jesus and the power of God explodes within our hearts, everything moves with the flow.

Jesus spoke to the Samaritan "woman at the well" in John 4. She had been married and divorced five times and was currently living with a man. (John 4:18) Her life was well acquainted with "beavers, fallen trees and a dammed-up life." She had only a testimony of shame and reproach. But

at that well, she met the dynamite of God, the Lord Jesus
Christ; and He blew that dam to smithereens! The rivers of
water started flowing in her life, and she initiated a citywide
revival. (John 4:39-42)

My friend, how is your river flowing? Got any fallen trees?
Remember, fallen trees attract beavers, and beavers dam up
lives. And dammed-up lives have no testimony.

Grace for the Race

"Wherefore lift up the hands which hang down, and the feeble knees; And make straight paths for your feet, lest that which is lame be turned out of the way; but let it rather be healed. Follow peace with all men, and holiness, without which no man shall see the Lord: Looking diligently lest any man fail of the grace of God; lest any root of bitterness springing up trouble you, and thereby many be defiled; Lest there be any fornicator, or profane person, as Esau, who for one morsel of meat sold his birthright. For ye know how that afterward, when he would have inherited the blessing, he was rejected: for he found no place of repentance, though he sought it carefully with tears" (Hebrews 12:12-17).

God's loving, caring hand in discipline has been extended in Hebrews 12:5-11. This discipline is exercised so that we may cooperate with God and realize His intentional purpose for our lives. Then the Hebrew writer, inspired by the Holy Spirit, follows the text on correction with a passage to encourage. God is full of grace and truth. Therefore, these two passages balance the scales: truth with discipline on the one side and grace with encouragement on the other side. This provides the balance we all need in life. If we are to build a spiritual testimony, we must balance the scales of our lives.

Likewise, we must strike the balance of knowledge and obedience. Knowing and believing are on one side of the coin of our lives, but on the other side is living and obeying. Hebrews 12 is a classic passage that not only teaches truth but also encourages us to live up to the truth. Hebrews 13:20-22 captures this thought in the concluding words of this great epistle:

> "Now the God of peace, that brought again from the dead our Lord Jesus, that great shepherd of the sheep, through the blood of the everlasting covenant, Make you perfect in every good work to do his will, working in you that which is well-pleasing in his sight, through Jesus Christ; to whom be glory forever and ever. Amen. And I beseech you, brethren, suffer the word of exhortation: for I have written a letter unto you in few words."

Truth that is known but not obeyed becomes a judgment on us rather than a help to us. James 4:17 summarizes this thought well:

> "Therefore to him that knoweth to do good, and doeth it not, to him it is sin."

I am convinced that more people know doctrinal truth than live doctrinal truth. We have an intellectual grasp of the doctrines of Scripture but know nothing of the practice of scriptural doctrine. However, unapplied doctrine is rendered worthless. Spiritual principles need explanation, illustration and exhortation; but unless they are applied, they become as salt that has lost its savor - useless! It has been said we understand the doctrines of grace but do not experience the grace of the doctrines.

The writer of Hebrews has been very much the teacher throughout this epistle, teaching us of the "better" way in Christ Jesus. Now he swaps roles and becomes the coach who exhorts us to press on toward the finish line:

> "...let us lay aside every weight, and the sin which doth so easily
> beset us, and let us run with patience the race that is set before us"
> (Hebrews 12:1).

We understand the doctrines of grace but do not experience the grace of the doctrines.

The discipline has been rigorous, and now each runner should become everything he or she has the potential of becoming as examples and testimonies to the lost. How can we do this? By the grace of God! Hebrews 12:12-17 instructs us about this "grace for the race" in three ways.

The Exhortation of Grace
The first thing in this exhortation is a *challenge* to help those who are weary, exhausted and feeble. There are three key phrases in verse twelve that illustrate this. The first phrase "lift up" means to set aright and to restore that which is in ruin. I am immediately reminded of the wall around Jerusalem that was destroyed and lay in ruins for 142 years until Nehemiah issued the challenge and lifted up the weary hands of his people to rebuild those walls. Discipline will make us strong, set things aright, and lift us up.

The second phrase in verse twelve is "hang down" which means to relax. For most of my adult life, I have jogged to stay in shape. As a runner, I know I need to pump my arms while jogging so that my upper body works in coordination with my lower body. But the longer I run and the more tired

I become, my arms start relaxing. They now dangle at my side and no longer work in coordination with my legs. That is why we must spiritually lift up, restore and set aright the hands which hang down.

It is my perspective that the church of the twenty-first century is relaxed and comfortable. Like many runners, I know many of us don't have to run too far before we're ready to quit. It reminds me of the man who was planning to run around his subdivision every day. After a month of running, someone asked him how he was doing. He replied, "Well, I'm up to the third mailbox now." Our churches, like this man, have become so comfortable. The church is not growing; the lost are not being won to Christ; and the sleepy saints are bragging about being up to the third mailbox in the race that is set before them. Vance Havner, the great preacher of yesteryear, once said, "I have come to comfort the afflicted and to afflict the comfortable." Dear friend, we will never accomplish the will of God with a relaxed, comfortable church! May God help the comfortable to get real uncomfortable!

> *We will never accomplish the will of God with a relaxed, comfortable church! May God help the comfortable to get real uncomfortable!*

We have lost our testimony to the world when they see no real, sustaining walk with the Lord Jesus Christ. Many lost people have been intrigued by Christianity enough to have considered it, and they have even attended church a few times. If we are to build a strong spiritual resume that will be noticed by a dying world, we must no longer "hang down." "Hang down" people cannot lift anyone else. Therefore, the world will die without ever knowing this "grace for the race."

The third phrase is "feeble knees." The Greek word used here for "feeble" means paralyzed. I am sorry to say this, but again this seems to portray the average church. And do you know why the church is paralyzed? Because individual Christians are paralyzed! Our knees have become so weary that we are crippled and cannot run our race. You see, when fatigue sets in, the arms droop and the legs wobble and the race is lost. Our challenge is to lift up our spiritually weak, weary and wobbly self by the grace that comes in God's deliverance and salvation. Isaiah said it well:

> "Strengthen ye the weak hands, and confirm the feeble knees. Say to them that are of a fearful heart, Be strong, fear not: behold, your God will come with vengeance, even God with a recompense; he will come and save you" (35:3-4).

Do you know why the church is paralyzed? Because individual Christians are paralyzed!

The Apostle Paul said it well to the Philippian church:

> "I can do all things through Christ which strengtheneth me" (Philippians 4:13).

> "But my God shall supply all your need according to his riches in glory by Christ Jesus" (Philippians 4:19).

The second thing we see in this exhortation of grace is *concern*. There is a great concern today because the case for Christianity has been weakened by our compromising lifestyles. Hebrews 12:13 instructs us to "make straight paths." The language here carries the idea of wheel tracks. The chariots of biblical times would leave a wheel track in the soil that one could follow. As Christians building a testimony, we ought to leave straight wheel tracks that can be easily followed by others. This means we need to stay in the lane God has chosen for us to run (as I alluded to in chapter three). Three things happen when we get out of our lane:

- We cut crooked paths for others to follow instead of "straight paths."

- We interfere with other runners and disqualify ourselves.

- We lose the race.

The principle of Proverbs 4:25-27 applies here:

> "Let thine eyes look right on, and let thine eyelids look straight before thee. Ponder the path of thy feet, and let all thy ways be established. Turn not to the right hand nor to the left: remove thy foot from evil."

Our spiritual resume depends on us staying in God's lane for our lives. The Adversary would have us to run in other lanes, evil lanes. The lane of money, the lane of sexual immorality, the lane of evil talk and the lane of selfishness has upended the testimony of many and renders us lame.

The phrase "turned out of the way" (Hebrews 12:13) means to be dislocated. When a wheel becomes dislocated, it leaves

a wobbly track, not a straight path. It then leads those following us to be shaky in their walk. A dislocated Christian
cannot be found faithful by those who follow.

Our spiritual resume depends on us staying in God's lane for our life.

Dislocation means to be lame.   Therefore, a dislocated
Christian is a limping, dysfunctional believer. Again, I think
of professing believers in Jesus Christ who are dislocated on
Sunday morning. Many are dislocated on Saturday night in
places no one would want to be when Jesus comes. But dislocated believers are most prevalent on Sunday night,
Wednesday night and soul-winning night.

The Explanation of Grace
Hebrews chapter twelve gives us some amazing truths about
sin:

- Verse 1 teaches that sin weighs us down.

- Verses 12-13 teach that sin cripples us.

- Verses 15-16 teach that sin will stop us.

So that sin and its consequences will not entangle us, our
text explains the work of grace in our lives. First, there is the
outward work of grace. We are to "follow peace with all men"
(verse 14). This deals with our human relationships. It
should be the goal of every blood-bought believer to live in
harmony and peace "with all men." I hear some proclaiming
that we should give peace a chance. But the Bible says we
are to give peace a chase! We are to "follow peace."

Recently, I was asked if I actually thought all those people at
the church really loved me. I responded by saying, "Well,
they're supposed to." I am not so naive that I believe they all
agree with me, but I do believe that they are to love me and I
am to love them and that we live in harmony with each
other. This is the Bible way. Now I understand it is not the
world's way or even the way it is in many churches, but it is
God's way.

> "Blessed are the peacemakers: for they shall be called the children
> of God" (Matthew 5:9).

> "If it be possible, as much as lieth in you, live peaceably with all
> men" (Romans 12:18).

> "Let us therefore follow after the things which make for peace, and
> things wherewith one may edify another" (Romans 14:19).

Our text also gives explanation to the *inward* work of grace.
We are to live in holiness. This deals with our heavenly relationship.

> "But as he which hath called you is holy, so be ye holy in all man-
> ner of conversation" (1 Peter 1:15).

Holiness means to live a pure, obedient life that is set apart for
God's glory. You cannot be holy without being pure and without being obedient. We are to be in this world in *contact* but
not in *conduct*. I also like to define holiness with one word -
different. We are to be different from others and the world.
Remember this truth: You cannot make a difference until you
are different! That is why I have selected to place my

Remember this truth: You cannot make
a difference until you are different!

own personal testimony as the first chapter of this book. God is different, and He made a difference in this ole Indian. Now that He's made a difference in me, I can make a difference in others. And His "grace for the race" is still making a difference in me.

God is holy and He is different - not in the weird and bizarre sense but because He is set apart from any other being. Some Christians who think holiness is being a weirdo have embarrassed me. They go around acting like some sanctimonious freak. I am amazed at some that must be so outlandish. One climbed a tower and said he was staying there until a certain amount of money came in that would continue to sponsor his program. I say let his program die! If God initiated it, then He will see it through; or else Philippians 1:6 and other passages are not true. God is an awesome, mighty, victorious God. He is not dependent on our little antics to hold His kingdom together. (That was a good place to say "Amen.")

Holiness is not only being set apart but also being set above.

Holiness is not only being set *apart* but also being set *above*. You see, holiness sets you above all the rest. It exalts you and lifts you up as an example. Holiness is a deliberate choice to seek cleansing from daily defilement and keeps your spiritual resume intact. This is why Hebrews 12:14 adds: "without which no man shall see the Lord." That, my friend, is a strong statement. Without pursuing peace and holiness, no one else will see God through your life. The reference is to unbelievers who observe our pursuit of peace and holiness. Without this pursuit, they will not be drawn to the Lord Jesus themselves. But through their observation of this chase in our lives, they will be pointed to the God of grace, thus obtaining "grace for the race" themselves.

Peace and holiness are so vital in leading unbelievers to a saving knowledge of Christ. Why? Because these are two of the greatest attributes of the Lord Himself. Christlikeness is the greatest point on any spiritual resume. This is why Paul wrote in Galatians 4:19:

> "My little children, of whom I travail in birth again until *Christ be formed in you*" (emphasis mine).

Paul said, "I labor over you like a woman giving birth, and I will continue in labor pain until Jesus is developed in you." The Hebrew writer said it this way: "looking diligently" (12:15). He's talking about taking a careful look at our life to see if we're feeble and crippled or if we're pursuing peace and holiness. If we're feeble and crippled, we have fallen short of the grace of God. Verse fifteen is not referring to falling from grace when it reads: "...lest any man fail of the grace of God." This passage is not about losing; it's about missing - missing God's best and God's opportunities. It means we lag behind in the spiritual race of life. God's grace deposits an unfathomable amount of potential in us. When we tap into His grace, we have all the potential and possibility that His power affords. This is why Paul proclaimed:

> "But by the grace of God I am what I am" (1 Corinthians 15:10).

Anything good in my life is due to the working of the grace of God. We are not manufacturers; we are distributors. He manufactures and deposits His grace within us. Then, and only then, we begin to distribute this grace in our life circumstances and to others. Wouldn't it be a tragedy to come to the end of life, look back on the years and see all kinds of missed opportunities?

We are not manufacturers; we are distributors.

Warning: Do not fail to be everything that grace can make you.

God's wonderful grace produces goodness in my life. As my friend Bill Stafford says, "Anything short of Hell is grace!" So we need to be careful to not squander this marvelous grace. Dear Christian, do not come to the end of your years only to realize the missed opportunities His grace affords. Don't look back on your race and see the losing effort with which you competed.

If we don't take a careful look, then we will live a careless life. Hebrews 12:15 goes on to tell us what happens to the person who does "fail of the grace of God." This person will have a "root of bitterness springing up." Satan wants to render you ineffective, and nothing does that better than a good dose of bitterness. This book could not contain the list of professing Christians who have quit church because they became bitter about something. "The carpet was the wrong color"; "the pews are not well padded"; "the church ran short of Sunday School quarterlies"; "our class had to change rooms," etc. You've heard the war stories enough to be familiar with all the excuses. The devil will use bitterness to suck the joy right out of you. Oftentimes, the Bible refers to bitterness as poison, and poison will destroy you and cut your life short. Verse fifteen gives two results of a bitter person:

- You will be troubled.

- You will defile many.

Bitterness is a self-inflicted wound. You shoot yourself. Taking on bitterness is to commit spiritual suicide. You don't even like yourself at this point - let alone anyone else. Bitterness (poison) gets in the very soul and heart of your life. The Hebrew writer speaks of it as a "root of bitterness." And anything in the root of a tree eventually spreads throughout the whole tree. Again, the language used in verse fifteen paints a picture for us: "...lest any root of bitterness springing up." Bitterness is at the "root" of life and has the power to spring upward in you. When bitterness has spread throughout you, your fruit is no longer tasteful, refreshing and nourishing. The fruit of bitterness replaces the fruit of the Spirit. The lost man then comes along and partakes of your bitter fruit. And what does he taste? Poison!

Bitterness is a self-inflicted wound. Taking on bitterness is to commit spiritual suicide.

"Looking diligently lest any man fail of the grace of God; lest any root of bitterness springing up trouble you, and *thereby many be defiled*" (Hebrews 12:15, emphasis mine).

Defiled means to dye or to stain. The picture here implies that the person who tastes of your fruit is stained or marked by your poor testimony. It means you have had a corrupt influence upon him. We need to maintain a careful look so as not to have a careless life!

The Example of Grace
The Bible gives Esau as a bad example of grace. He is one who chose to neglect grace, and thus, was disqualified in the race. His spiritual resume was ruined by one bad decision. Dear friend, please understand that one ungodly decision can destroy an otherwise perfect spiritual resume. Esau made a decision based on *present gratification* rather than *future satisfaction*. Esau's uncommitment to godliness negated any hope he had in the race.

> ## *His spiritual resume was ruined by one bad decision.*

He was *uncommitted sensually*. Verse sixteen calls him a "fornicator." A fornicator is an immoral person. Esau's commitment was to satisfying his physical desires and not living pure. Jacob was his brother and Isaac his father, but yet he did not know God. Esau knew about God, but he did not know God. He had great light. He had heard the promises of God. Yet, with determined willfulness, he turned his back on God and the things of God.

Esau reminds me of many today who come from godly homes. They have seen the Christian life fleshed out in the life of a relative. Many have been raised in church and have been taught the ways of God. They know about God, but do they really know God? They may even attend church and carry a Bible under their arm, but do they practice its teachings? Many claim to be saved but yet are involved in pornography and adultery. They have become like our society - tolerant of everything. They portray themselves as believers but are devoid of truth. It appears to this preacher that our society has tasted their fruit "and thereby many be defiled."

Esau also was *uncommitted spiritually*. The Bible says he was a "profane person." This means he had no reverence for the things of God. He rendered those things unhallowed and unsacred. He treated spiritual things as being of no account. Simply put, there just wasn't enough room for God in his life. Now there may have been room for church; but somewhere along the line, God got shoved out of his life. You see, the highest call upon your life is not your *role* in the church (as important as that is) but your *relationship* with Christ! Esau wanted the role without the relationship. He wanted God's presents more than God's presence!

He wanted God's presents more than God's presence!

The scripture says that Esau "sold his birthright." He sold out only to be left out! Hebrews 12:17 instructs that "he would have inherited the blessing." He could have been the primary person through whom the great spiritual blessings were to come, but he sold out. And he sold out cheap - for a bowl of beef stew! He sold out for the moment and lost all eternity. When he finally came to his senses, it was too late. Esau stands as a reminder of one who lightly valued spiritual realities and threw away a golden opportunity. He is the prime example of: "lest any man fail of the grace of God . . ."

In conclusion, let me give two admonitions. Adults, bring your children up in the "nurture and admonition of the Lord" (Ephesians 6:4). Encourage them to be sold out to Christ. They will definitely sell out to something. Your greatest contribution to them will be your own godly walk with the Lord. Give them this book, and let them read this chapter; for their whole race is still in front of them. I am afraid that our children do not see in us or hear from us the things of God, as they should.

I remember a family who had a wayward son. They grieved over his rebellion and sin. One day this young man was gloriously saved. He was on fire, and he was a soul-winner. His parents had some dignitaries over for dinner one night and asked their son to pray over the meal. He did so; but before praying, he asked each of those dignitaries about their personal relationship with the Lord Jesus. This was embarrassing to his parents. Upon hearing this, I remembered how they anguished over this son when he was a rebel and pleaded with God to change him. Now that God had performed a work of grace in him, they felt he was "too religious." Parents, give yourself and your children **wholly** to the Lord.

Young people, live for Jesus **right now.** You have opportunities to touch people now that you will never have again. The idea of sowing wild oats while you're young is of the devil. Sin **always** leaves its scars. Remember, the tears of adulthood don't undo the foolish choices of youth (just ask Esau).

Remember, the tears of adulthood don't undo the foolish choices of youth (just ask Esau).

It is so important to make the right decisions throughout *all* of life. Don't pursue those things which have no eternal value. The challenge of giving an account to God one day will be seeing what we have done in comparison to what we could have done.

God's Others

As Christians we have our own personal, individual testimonies. But we also have a collective testimony as the Church of the Lord Jesus. This collective testimony is built by our individual testimonies. However, our collective testimony does affect our individual testimonies.

Let me illustrate. When you come together with your local congregation on Sunday morning, you bring your individual testimony with you. As you identify and associate with the local church, you form a testimony that combines your testimony with their testimonies. The combined testimonies of you and others form the church's testimony in the community. The church's testimony then becomes a part of your own.

How often have you heard a christian say they belong to a certain church only to have someone respond, "Is that where ole So-and-So attends?" Then they expound on the evilness of this person. Like it or not, your testimony as a member of that church is affected by "ole So-and-So."

Likewise, your testimony is enhanced when your church and individuals within it maintain a good report within your community. We need to understand that "God's others" do impact our testimony and reputation in our community. That is why church discipline is taught in the Bible.

Hebrews 11:35-40 illustrates the importance and impact of "God's others":

> "Women received their dead raised to life again: and *others* were tortured, not accepting deliverance; that they might obtain a better resurrection: And *others* had trial of cruel mockings and scourgings, yea, moreover of bonds and imprisonment: They were stoned, they were sawn asunder, were tempted, were slain with the sword: they wandered about in sheepskins and goatskins; being destitute, afflicted, tormented; (Of whom the world was not worthy:) they wandered in deserts, and in mountains, and in dens and caves of the earth. And these all, having obtained a good report through faith, received not the promise: God having provided some better thing for us, that they without us should not be made perfect." (italics mine)

The "others" in this text refer to men and women of everyday life who were not necessarily leaders but who had one distinctive trait: they believed God! This passage pictures men and women doing what God demanded by exercising a strong faith in God. These "others" did the impossible; they placed their testimony for God above all earthly ties and joys - even to the point of surrendering their lives in death.

It is amazing how "God's others" encourage us in our walk with God. Consider Elijah in 1 Kings 19. Conflicts with Ahab and Jezebel had wreaked discouragement and vexation of spirit. Verse nine tells us he had come to a cave; and the Lord asked him, "What doest thou here, Elijah?" God then asks the same question in verse thirteen. Elijah answers in verse fourteen:

> "I have been very jealous for the LORD God of hosts: because the

children of Israel have forsaken thy covenant, thrown down thine
altars, and slain thy prophets with the sword; and I, even I only,
am left; and they seek my life, to take it away."

Elijah is fearful for his very life. The spiritual status of his
nation is at an all-time low. The people have forsaken God
and His Word and are killing His prophets. God then
answers Elijah in such an encouraging manner:

> "Yet I have left me seven thousand in Israel, all the knees which
> have not bowed unto Baal, and every mouth which hath not
> kissed him." (v. 18)

Wow! Seven thousand others who are on His side. It is no
wonder the next verse reads: "So he (Elijah) departed
thence..." No longer did he need the hideaway of a cave. He
could now move forward and live zealously for God.

I have found there is strength in numbers. Now I know God
sometimes requires us to take a stand on our own. But He
has surrounded us with "others" for the sake of strengthen-
ing and encouraging. Oh, how we need "others"! When "others" come along-side of us, we live more aggressively for God
and less passively. Ecclesiastes 4:9-12 says it best:

> "Two are better than one; because they have a good reward for
> their labor. For if they fall, the one will lift up his fellow: but woe
> to him that is alone when he falleth; for he hath not another to
> help him up. Again, if two lie together, then they have heat: but
> how can one be warm alone? And if one prevail against him, two
> shall withstand him; and a threefold cord is not quickly broken."

Others That Stood Faithful

Chapter eleven of Hebrews makes a distinctive transition in
verse thirty-five. Up to this point, the writer gives testimony
of the faithful who were rescued from danger. However, in

verse thirty-five, a change is made when the writer says, "...and others were tortured, not accepting deliverance..." With the first group, we praise God in their deliverance; with the second group, we praise God in their deaths. The first group escaped by God's grace; the second group endured by God's grace. "Others" represent a unique group. This "Hall of Faith" chapter mentions God's unlikely, God's unexpected and now exposes God's unnamed.

Not only do the faithful stand; the faithful stand out. A person of faith has a noticeable aura about them. Hebrews 11:35 lists three distinguishable traits of the faithful others.

Not only do the faithful stand; the faithful stand out.

• Their Danger

The text says they "were tortured." The word comes from the Greek root for *kettledrum*. It refers to a person having their arms and legs stretched over a large drum-like instrument and then, like a drum, being beat upon repeatedly with clubs. The purpose of the beating was for those tortured to renounce Christ. Can't you just see these persecuted being asked to renounce their faith only to shout among their groanings the testimony of the New Testament Christian: "Jesus Christ is Lord!" They would withstand all the tortures of the world in order to keep their witness untainted. These "others" could proclaim with the Apostle Paul: "...I bear in my body the marks of the Lord Jesus" (Galatians 6:17).

We are fortunate in God-blessed America to escape such torture. We run the danger of personal rejection, but we do not know the physical torture of these heroes of the faith. Yet there are parts of our world where Christians are physically persecuted and interrogated for their faith. I have visited parts of our world where such fear exists.

• Their Decision

"God's others" "were tortured, *not accepting deliverance*" (italics mine). This indicates they were threatened and then offered the opportunity to renounce Christ and save their own hide. But God's faithful were willing to be beaten to death rather than compromise the testimony of "Christ in you, the hope of glory" (Colossians 1:27).

As I think of these brave, faithful "others," I am moved with much awe and respect. I want to shout to the top of my lungs: "Thanks be unto God for those who will not give up, back up, shut up or let up until they've been taken up!" O, to God that we had more church members like these unnamed martyrs! They had no platforms, but they did have passion. They possessed no positions, but their position in Christ did possess them! On Earth we will not know their names, but in Heaven these "others" will shine as trophies of God's marvelous grace.

They had no platforms, but they did have passion. They possessed no positions, but their position in Christ did possess them!

As I think about their decision to suffer persecution for Jesus' sake, I cannot but consider what I would decide if given the same choice - to be able to join these and Paul to say:

> "I am crucified with Christ: nevertheless I live; *yet not I*, but Christ liveth in me: and the life which I now live in the flesh I live by the faith of the Son of God, who loved me, and gave himself for me." (Galatians 2:20, italics mine)

"God's others" made the decision that they would live in the realm of "yet not I." I find that very few of us live in this domain. Why? Because we pursue *our* domain. We must decide to let Christ live in us.

• Their Destiny

It is your destiny that keeps you intact. The destiny of "God's others" was "a better resurrection." They would not sacrifice the future on the altar of the immediate. They preferred being put to death because by faith they knew that one day they would be resurrected to eternal life.

They would not sacrifice the future on the altar of the immediate.

The destination "better resurrection" implies there is a "worse resurrection." Revelation 20:11-15 describes the "worse resurrection" as "the second death":

> "And I saw a great white throne, and him that sat on it, from whose face the earth and the heaven fled away; and there was found no place for them. And I saw the dead, small and great, stand before God; and the books were opened: and another book was opened, which is the book of life: and the dead were judged out of those things which were written in the books, according to their works.

> And the sea gave up the dead which were in it; and death and hell
> delivered up the dead which were in them: and they were judged
> every man according to their works. And death and hell were cast
> into the lake of fire. This is the second death. And whosoever was
> not found written in the book of life was cast into the lake of fire."

I think of the people today who are willing to lose their God-directed destiny on the altar of the immediate. Like Esau, we are selling our future for a bowl of pottage. I think of the man who sacrifices his family and his future for a fling with a strange woman. I think of a teenage girl who forfeits her future for a passionate moment with her boyfriend. I think of a young, successful executive who surrenders untapped potential for the pleasure of drugs and alcohol. Don't let your today ruin your tomorrow!

Don't let your today ruin your tomorrow!

Often I am asked, "Pastor, don't you believe that if people have enough faith that God will rescue them from death, sickness, hardship, etc.?" Not necessarily. If He does, then we have a theological problem in Hebrews 11. This chapter is about those who had faith, yet God did not deliver all of them. The three Hebrew boys that were thrown in the furnace because they would not bow to the golden image made by King Nebuchadnezzar illustrate the possibility of deliverance and the possibility of death. The king decreed that they would be thrown into the furnace if they would not worship his god and gave them a chance to retreat their position. But they answered:

> "O Nebuchadnezzar, we are not careful to answer thee in this matter. If it be so, our God whom we serve is able to deliver us from the burning fiery furnace, and he will deliver us out of thine hand,

O king. But if not, be it known unto thee, O king, that we will not
serve thy gods, nor worship the golden image which thou hast set
up." (Daniel 3:16-18)

Another example is found in Acts 12. Peter was in prison
awaiting his execution day when the church prayed and he
was delivered out of jail by the angel. Many use this passage as
proof that faith will rescue you, but hold on a minute. Stop the
tape, hit the rewind button and stop at Acts 12:1-2. Now play.

"Now about that time Herod the king stretched forth his hands to
vex certain of the church. And he killed James the brother of John
with the sword."

The Apostle James died, while the Apostle Peter was delivered. Why? Because of faith? No. In faith James died; in
faith Peter was spared. John 21:22 indicates it is left up to the
sovereignty of God.

One last example and then I will leave it alone. What about
Stephen, the deacon? The Bible says he was a man "full of
faith and power" (Acts 6:8), yet God allowed him to be stoned
to death. Picture the scene with me. Stephen had just
preached a sermon to unbelieving Jews who "were cut to the
heart" by his message. They took him with the intention of
persecuting him. They may have asked him to renounce
Christ and then they would release him. But about that
time, he "looked up steadfastly into heaven, and saw the
glory of God, and Jesus standing on the right hand of God"
(Acts 7:55). Therefore, he says, "Behold, I see the heavens
opened, and the Son of man standing on the right hand of
God" (Acts 7:56). Now I realize I've inserted a little of my
imagination here. But the point is that Stephen was a man
"full of faith" and yet was not delivered from his persecutors.

What did God do for Stephen you may ask? He gave him the grace to persevere amid persecution - even to the point of praying a prayer of forgiveness for his murderers. He then gave Stephen a standing ovation! He taught Stephen that when you stand up for Jesus, He will stand up for you! You see, sometimes faith gets you out of trouble; and sometimes it gets you into trouble! George Duffield, Jr. must have had Stephen in mind when he wrote these lyrics:

> *Stand up, stand up for Jesus, Ye soldiers of the cross;*
> *Lift high his royal banner, It must not suffer loss:*
> *From victory unto victory His army shall he lead,*
> *Till every foe is vanquished, And Christ is Lord indeed.*[1]

Sometimes faith gets you out of trouble; and sometimes it gets you into trouble!

Others That Suffered Faithfully

Hebrews 11:36 mentions yet another group of "others":

> "And others had trial of cruel mockings and scourgings, yea, moreover of bonds and imprisonment."

The first set of "others" stood faithfully; this group of "others" suffered faithfully. They first suffered in mental trials through "cruel mockings." This means they were ridiculed, insulted, treated with contempt and cursed. They were sarcastically attacked. This is so relevant to what is happening today. Christians are being so ridiculed and mocked in the workplace, at school, and in the marketplace that we have been silenced. Our silence has been the objective of the liberal crowd that is attempting to erase God from our memory. And it ain't gonna get any better! We live in such a tolerant society that if a person speaks out against homosexuality or a lack of moral integrity in the White House he is viewed as a narrow-minded bigot and may be brought to litigation for hate crimes. Our society has become so comfortable with evil that even professing Christians are taken by all the hogwash. These mental battles are waged in hopes of intimidating and silencing the witness of born-again believers. I'm telling you that "cruel mockings" and mental trials have been well-used weaponry of the devil for millenniums.

Secondly, they suffered in physical torture. They were scourged like the Lord Jesus was by the Roman soldiers that crucified Him. To be scourged was to be beaten with rods, whips and cords of leather with bone and metal chips tied to the end. They were chained. Their arms and legs bore the sores and scars from the metal bands rubbing and digging into their flesh. They were imprisoned in rat-infested jails.

A couple of years ago, I had the privilege of ministering in Cuba. I was overwhelmed by the fact that most of these Cuban pastors had been imprisoned for several years because of their testimony. I was so humbled yet so honored by their desire for me to minister to them. Why? "Remember them that are in bonds, as bound with them..." (Hebrews 13:3).

Hebrews 11:37 continues the story of those "others" that suffered faithfully:

> "They were stoned, they were sawn asunder, were tempted, were slain with the sword: they wandered about in sheepskins and goatskins; being destitute, afflicted, tormented."

As I read that, I am overtaken by the fact that their love relationship with Jesus was so precious that their testimony for Him was non-negotiable - even to the point of martyrdom. Tradition teaches that Isaiah was sawn in two for his faith. Others were afflicted beyond reason. Talk about human rights; they didn't even enjoy the same decency that an animal would receive! They were deprived of the basic necessities of life. The word "tempted" means to be lured. It reminds me of the ploy of Satan even today. Christians are constantly being lured via television, movies, magazines, etc.

> *Their love relationship with Jesus was so precious that their testimony for Him was non-negotiable - even to the point of martyrdom.*

Thirdly, they sustained a spiritual testimony. Don't miss this - God developed a spiritual testimony using the mental trials and physical torture. It never ceases to amaze me how God takes what was intended for harm and uses it for good. I guess that's why He's God and I'm John! Praise be to His name! He takes the ugly and makes it beautiful. He takes the pain and creates much gain. He's God!

The Word of God gives a most incredible statement about "God's others": **"Of whom the world was not worthy"** (Hebrews 11:38). They were rejected by society but received by the Savior! The world despised them, but God delighted in them. They were such magnificent people that, according to God, they were too good to remain in such a wicked world. Many may not have thought much of their testimony, but God did! You may think that your testimony doesn't count for much on Earth, but it sure counts for something in Heaven.

They were rejected by society but received by the Savior!

All These Sacrificed the Immediate for the Future

Someone once said, "A faith that falters before the finish had a flaw from the first." In Hebrews 11:35-40, not one name is mentioned. We simply know this group as "God's others." Why they are not named individually I do not know. But it does make me consider this: How many "others" are heroes of the faith that we know nothing about today? What about that missionary in some remote area who is faithfully sharing the Good News of Jesus Christ? What about the ole country preacher in the Appalachian Mountains? What about the dear senior adult lady that has been teaching the first grade Sunday School class for forty-three years? It's apparent to me that God still has His "others."

Near Washington D.C., there is a monument in memory of all the unknown soldiers who gave their lives for their country. Hundreds of unmarked graves are found in Arlington Cemetery. Each of those graves is marked with a simple white cross - no tombstone, no birthday or death date engraved and no name listed. Each of those heroes had a mom and dad. Perhaps they had a wife, children and brothers and sisters. They were known and loved in life but have died with no name. We could say they were our nation's "others." We enjoy our freedom and lifestyle today because of those brave, strong individuals.

Hebrews 11:35-40 is our spiritual "Arlington Cemetery." Here we also find brave, strong and nameless individuals who paved spiritual paths upon which we still walk. These also were soldiers who laid down their lives for the cause of spiritual freedom. We find the *Tomb of the Unknown Soldier* in Arlington Cemetery. We find the *Testimonies of the Unnamed Saints* in the "Arlington Cemetery" of this passage.

Two points that surface concerning these unnamed martyrs:

1. The first is the legacy they left. Hebrews 11:39 states:

> "And these all, having obtained a good report..."

"God's others" had left the legacy of a good testimony! The word "obtained" signifies that it was earned. It did not come easy but came by the shedding of their blood. They died with God's stamp of approval upon them, and the Holy Spirit made sure the Hebrew writer penned these words down for us. Knowing that we are right before God gives us the strength to accept all that is wrong from men! Hebrews 11:39 ends with this phrase:

> "...received not the promise."

Knowing that we are right before God gives us the strength to accept all that is wrong from men!

These heroes believed *before* the promise was fulfilled in Christ. They had the *shadow* and lived by faith. How dare we who have the *substance* draw back. We live on the "after side" of Calvary and the empty tomb. This makes their legacy all the more intriguing.

2. The second is the loyalty they exhibited. Hebrews 11:40 reads:

> "God having provided some better thing for us, that they without us should not be made perfect."

We are far more privileged today than they were. The death, burial and resurrection of Jesus Christ is a historic fact. But it was not until our time, the time of Christianity, that their salvation could be completed and made perfect. Until Jesus' atoning work on the cross was finished, salvation was incomplete - no matter how great the faith. Their salvation was anticipated, ours accomplished; their atonement was based on what Christ would do, ours on what He has done.

I carry a picture of Janet in my day timer. As I travel I am often asked to show a picture of my wife if she is not with me. As I show her picture, I think how I would like to have her with me. The picture is a nice reminder, but it cannot replace the real person. "God's others" lived with a picture of Calvary, but He has "provided some better thing for us." This is why they could not be "made perfect" without us. Therefore, we join the army of God to expand the troops of "God's others."

Passing the Torch

Every four years the Olympics are initiated with many athletes participating in a ceremony of running several miles while carrying the Olympic torch. Each runner proudly runs his distance, holding high the flaming torch. After he has successfully run his course, he passes the torch to the next athlete who anxiously waits his turn.

We are to build our spiritual resume so that our testimony outlives us and touches others. I want to reiterate a thought from chapter two: Our testimony is the only thing we leave that has staying power. I remember the excitement the Olympics brought to Atlanta in 1996. However, the burning torch that the athletes carried with pride was the only thing that remained when the games were over and everyone had gone home. Our testimony will live in the hearts of our loved ones long after they have spent the inheritance we left them. Our good testimony will live in their thoughts, attitudes, beliefs and actions until they die. Your testimony will have more influence on them than the money you leave. It will have more impact on them than the possessions you leave. It will have more impression on them than the business you leave. Why? Because your money, possessions and business

cannot be imitated; but your testimony can be! Your testimony can live in anyone, at anytime, in any place and in any
social-economic situation.

Little children used to sing: "Give me oil in my lamp. Keep it
burning." I want to have oil burning in my torch when I pass
out of this world. I want to pass a brightly burning torch on
to the next generation. I have noticed that children and

Your money, possessions and business cannot be imitated; but your testimony can be!

youth pay particular attention to the inconsistencies of our
lives. I do not want them to see in Johnny Hunt a torch that
is charred and long since extinguished. That is why I love the
man Joshua so much. He, like the Apostle Paul, could say, "I
have fought a good fight, I have finished my course, I have
kept the faith" (2 Timothy 4:7).

Joshua pulls Israel's leaders together in Joshua chapter twenty-three. He is setting the stage for the passing of the torch.
He will give his charge to them and then pass his torch on to
the whole nation in chapter twenty-four. At his leadership
meeting sits the distinguished men of Israel. There is Caleb,
his beloved friend, the one who was with him in giving the
favorable report to Moses to go possess the land. Some sev-
enty years have passed since that time, but he and Caleb's
torch has not flickered out. There sits Phinehas, the son of
Eleazar the priest, the spiritual leader of the people. Also sitting there are the courageous soldiers who have fought

valiantly with Joshua through seven years of campaigns. It is some fifteen to twenty years since the conquest and distribution of the land. Joshua now summons Israel's best to warn them of the dangers that lurk if they depart from the Lord God. He is an old man and will soon die at the age of 110. But before he does, Joshua wants to take them on a trip down memory lane. He speaks of God's unfailing faithfulness and goodness. He magnifies God's presence, protection and power on their behalf. His charge: "You be faithful and good as well."

Joshua never forgot God's blessings; he never got over His care. He is now "waxed old and stricken in age" (Joshua 23:1). Looking back over his life, he sees how God touched him with His good hand and blessed him with His good land. Joshua had been serving God for a long time, but he did not have a short memory. So many of us Christians live with a short memory. We forget God's goodness every time something goes awry. I have seen numerous people helped by

So many of us Christians live with a short memory. We forget God's goodness every time something goes awry.

others or the church soon turn on them. I am grateful that Joshua left the testimony of a grateful person. I hope I may live as Joshua. I pray I never live long enough to forget the good hand of God upon my life. I could still be back in that poolroom cussing and drinking. But thanks be to God for His good hand! I could still be living outside the love, care and friendship of a local church. But thanks be to God for His good land!

The testimony Joshua left with these Jewish leaders was full of reminders of the blessings of God. I think Joshua knew that dwelling on the blessings of God was strong motivation for obedience. Therefore, he will remind them of God's blessings in four distinct ways in Joshua chapter twenty-three.

The Work of God

Joshua's God was busy at work on their behalf. First, he recounts the work of God as seen through His *deliverance.*

> "...that the LORD had given rest unto Israel from all their enemies" (v. 1).

> "And ye have seen all that the LORD your God hath done unto all these nations because of you; for the LORD your God is he that hath fought for you" (v. 3).

Joshua's walk down memory lane most assuredly included the drowning of the Egyptian army. His mind's eye could still see the chariot wheels of the Egyptian soldiers marring up in the mud after they had crossed on dry ground. He could still see the parted waters crashing in on the Egyptians. I'm sure he remembered the floating helmets of the soldiers as they rushed downstream and the dead bodies of a once invincible foe washing to the riverbanks. I believe Joshua must have surely shouted about this time in his presentation!

I suppose in the theatre of his mind he saw the victory over the Amalekites. Moses had told Joshua to choose men to fight Amalek while he stood on the hilltop with the rod of God outstretched. Moses' hands grew weary; and each time he lowered the rod of God, the Amalekites prevailed in battle. Therefore, Aaron and Hur held his hands up until the victory was secured (Exodus 17:12). Joshua's ears still tingled with the words of Moses:

> "And the LORD said unto Moses, Write this for a memorial in a book, and rehearse it in the ears of Joshua: for I will utterly put out the remembrance of Amalek from under heaven" (Exodus 17:14).

Secondly, he recalls the work of God as seen through His *distribution*. Israel had gained control of the land of Canaan, but there still remained territory to possess and pockets of resistance to overcome. But God had divided the remaining nations among the twelve tribes of Israel as an inheritance and promised to eventually drive them out of the land.

I think every born-again Christian can relate to this. God has delivered us by His good hand and placed us in His good land to possess it and enjoy it. However, there are still some pockets of resistance to overcome. God saved me on January 7, 1973 and delivered me out of the land of bondage. He then moved me into the promised land. However, I'm still fighting to overcome the pockets of resistance in my life. I have some foreign things in my life that I have to resist. But if I'm obedient, they eventually will be wiped out. That pocket of pride will be wiped away, and humility will dwell in the land. The pocket of greed will be wiped out and replaced by a giving spirit. The pocket of temper will be expelled, and temperance will permeate the land. The pocket of bitterness will be ejected, and peace will be embraced. As we walk faithfully with the Lord, one victory will follow another.

The great danger that the people of Israel faced was a gradual shift in attitude toward the pagan nations that caused them to start accepting their ways and imitating them. This

is the same problem with the average Christian today. We
are glad to be saved and delivered out of our Egypt. We move
into the bountiful land of Canaan. We live obediently to the
commands of Almighty God. But then one day, we start
accepting and imitating the way of the world.

The Christian's greatest struggle today in God-blessed
America is our gradual shift in attitude toward accepting the
ways of our society. Our imminent danger lies in this fact:
What we accept today we will embrace tomorrow! The torch
that has been passed down in our great land from generation
to generation is becoming more degenerate. We keep seeing
a "degeneration of our generations." The torch we are passing down keeps losing her brilliance and illumination. I
believe this is the problem that the Lord Jesus saw with the
church at Ephesus:

What we accept today
we will embrace tomorrow!

> "I know thy works, and thy labor, and thy patience, and how thou
> canst not bear them which are evil: and thou hast tried them
> which say they are apostles, and are not, and hast found them
> liars: And hast borne, and hast patience, and for my name's sake
> hast labored, and hast not fainted. Nevertheless I have somewhat
> against thee, because thou hast left thy first love. Remember
> therefore from whence thou are fallen, and repent, and do thy first
> works; or else I will come unto thee quickly, *and will remove thy
> candlestick out of his place*, except thou repent" (Revelation 2:2-5,
> emphasis mine).

Tolerance is the buzzword of the day. One is perceived as
mean-spirited, judgmental and even cruel if he is not toler-

ant of the offenses of others. Dr. R. G. Lee is the late, great pastor of Bellevue Baptist Church in Memphis. He was a great orator who once addressed the issue of a truth-pro-claiming preacher being considered mean and cruel: "I know some people call the preacher who stands squarely upon the preaching of Christ and His apostles narrow, harsh and cruel. As to being narrow, I have no desire to be any broader than was Jesus. As to being cruel, is it cruel to tell a man the truth? Is a man to be called cruel who declares the whole counsel of God and points out to men their danger? Is it cruel to arouse sleeping people to the fact that the house is on fire? Is it cruel to jerk a blind man away from the rat-tlesnake and its coil? Is it cruel to declare to people the deadliness of disease and to tell them which medicine to take?" And then he concluded with this powerful statement: "I had rather be called cruel for being kind than to be called kind for being cruel!"

Joshua warned his leadership team of accepting and tolerat-ing the ways of the foreign nations still dwelling in the land:

> "That ye come not among these nations, these that remain among you..." (Joshua 23:7).

Joshua knew that a gradual shift toward tolerance would put their torch out:

> "Else if ye do in any wise go back, and cleave unto the remnant of these nations, even these that remain among you, and shall make marriages with them, and go in unto them, and they to you: Know for a certainty that the LORD your God will no more drive out any of these nations from before you; but they shall be snares and traps unto you, and scourges in your sides, and thorns in your eyes, until ye perish from off this good land which the LORD your God hath given you" (23:12-13).

The third thing Joshua remembered about the work of God was His *devotion*. He spoke of God's work on their behalf in Joshua chapter twenty-three:

> "...the LORD had given rest unto Israel from all *their* enemies..." (v. 1).

> "And ye have seen all that the LORD *your* God hath done..." (v. 3a).

> "...for the LORD *your* God is he that hath fought for *you*" (v. 3b).

> "And the LORD *your* God, he shall expel them from before *you*..." (v. 5a).

> "...as the LORD *your* God hath promised unto *you*" (v. 5b). (emphasis mine)

Joshua kept showing these national leaders the devotion and dedication that God had for them. He also emphasized the personal nature of their relationship with God with the continual use of "the LORD *your* God." Joshua kept pointing them to God's good hand upon them. He did not fall into the trap of self-elevation. He was a humble man who knew why the blessings were flowing. He did not say, "Since I have been your leader..." Elevation of self is the most natural thing to do. In fact, it was the demise of Lucifer.

> "How art thou fallen from heaven, O Lucifer, son of the morning! how art thou cut down to the ground, which·didst weaken the nations! For thou hast said in thine heart, *I will* ascend into heaven, *I will* exalt my throne above the stars of God: *I will* sit also upon the mount of the congregation, in the sides of the north *I will* ascend above the heights of the clouds; *I will* be like the most High. Yet thou shalt be brought down to hell, to the sides of the pit" (Isaiah 14:12-15, emphasis mine).

Ezekiel informs us that Satan was "perfect" in his ways from the day he was created "till iniquity was found" in him (Ezekiel 28:15). What was this iniquity? Self-elevation! The natural thing to do is to promote yourself and talk about your accomplishments. But Joshua would not fall into that trap. He knew "from whence cometh my help" (Psalm 121:1).

> "For they got not the land in possession by their own sword, neither did their own arm save them: but thy right hand, and thine arm, and the light of thy countenance, because thou hadst a favor unto them" (Psalm 44:3).

Joshua knew a truth that was not yet written. In fact, the Spirit of God has greatly admonished me with this same timeless truth:

> "If ye will not hear, and if ye will not lay it to heart, to give glory unto my name, saith the LORD of hosts, I will even send a curse upon you, *and I will curse your blessings:* yea, I have cursed them already, because ye do not lay it to heart" (Malachi 2:2, emphasis mine).

Joshua wanted to make sure that the leaders of Israel understood who got the glory. I want to do the same. In fact, I want to use this book to give God the glory for what He has done in my life. He, and He alone, deserves all the glory and honor. I want to pass on the torch of God someday; therefore, I'd better understand the work of God and give Him the glory for it. But I better also understand...

The Word of God

The work of God needs to be understood in order to pass on a hot, glowing torch but so too does the Word of God. Joshua chapter twenty-three gives us four main words concerning the Word of God. The first word from the Word is *courage.*

> "Be ye therefore very courageous to keep and to do all that is writ-

ten in the book of the law of Moses, that ye turn not aside there-
from to the right hand or to the left" (v. 6).

If we are to pass on the torch to others, we must not turn
away from the teachings of the Bible. And if we are to stay
true to the Bible, we must have *courage*. It takes courage to
defy the crowd. It takes courage to obey God. It takes
courage to stand on the truth. It may take courage to fight,
to go to war, to do battle with your enemy; but it takes even

If we are to pass on the torch to others, we must not turn away from the teachings of the Bible.

greater courage to obey! This is the lesson Samuel had to
teach King Saul when he was disobedient to God. You will
remember that God had commanded Saul to completely
destroy the Amalekites:

> "Thus saith the LORD of hosts, I remember that which Amalek did to
> Israel, how he laid wait for him in the way, when he came up from
> Egypt. Now go and smite Amalek, and utterly destroy all that they
> have, and spare them not; but slay both man and woman, infant
> and suckling, ox and sheep, camel and ass" (1 Samuel 15:2-3).

Saul decided to spare King Agag and the choice animals. As
a result, God sent Samuel, the prophet of God, to confront
Saul about his disobedience. Saul excused himself and his
poor decision by stating that the animals were to be used as
sacrifices offered to God. At this point he has made a pious
sounding defense of his actions. But Samuel's reply pierced
through the religious verbiage with this condemnation:

> "Hath the LORD as great delight in burnt offerings and sacrifices, as

in obeying the voice of the LORD? Behold, to obey is better than
sacrifice, and to hearken than the fat of rams" (1 Samuel 15:22).

Saul had courage to battle his foe. He was willing to fight
hand-to-hand combat with his enemy, but he did not have
the courage to be obedient to the Word of God. It is true that
sacrifice is needed today; but if we are earnest about building a spiritual resume and passing on the torch, then we better get serious about obedience! Those who obey God often
will be ridiculed, lose friends or suffer persecution.

I want to challenge each of you to make the Bible visible in
your everyday life. You businessmen ought to have a copy
on your desk and keep it in plain view for all to see. You students ought to carry it with you to class. You construction
workers ought to have a copy in your lunch box. If you don't
have the courage to display the Bible, you won't have the

If you don't have the courage to display the Bible, you won't have the courage to dispense the Bible!

courage to dispense the Bible! I've seen men with protrud-
ing biceps that are bigger than my leg who have spiritual
muscles infected with polio. They will stand up for their
rights but never stand up for what is right.

The first chapter of this book, *Out of the Poolroom*, has been
printed in booklet form. My dentist, Dr. John Peacock, has
copies of it in his waiting room. He also has children's bible
story books, a book on hymnology and other Christian liter-
ature. He has the courage to display Christian material; and

by so doing, he is portraying a Christlike testimony to all of his patients.

The second word from the Word is *conformity.* Now it is true that we are to live in this world in contact but never in conduct:

> "That ye come not among these nations, these that remain among you; neither make mention of the name of their gods, nor cause to swear by them, neither serve them, nor bow yourselves unto them" (Joshua 23:7).

Did you notice the progression of their conformity?

- Association: "...come not among these nations..."

- Apathy: "...neither make mention of the name of their gods..."

- Acclamation: "...nor cause to swear by them..."

- Apostasy: "...neither serve them..."

- Adoration: "...nor bow yourselves unto them."

What started out innocently ended insidiously. Compromise always ends up being a casket. This is the ultimate plan of Satan. He desires to move the people of God into a slow, gradual decline until he has snared his prey. His plan calls for

Compromise always ends up being a casket.

the world to bow at his feet and worship him. Seduction is always silent, and deception is always deadly. So take notice: When you kneel at the altar of humanity, you may never get up!

The third word from the Word is *commitment*. We are to be totally committed to the Word of God. If not, our spiritual resume will be without any references. Who would be willing to refer to you as one whose torch is on fire if there is no commitment? Even the world asks for commitment! Joshua said:

> "But cleave unto the LORD your God, as ye have done unto this day" (Joshua 23:8).

To "cleave" means to be firmly attached to something. It pictures two objects being glued together and, thus inseparable. If our relationship to Christ is such, there will be great loyalty and steadfastness to Him. Joshua commended the national leaders because they had done that up to this point. His admonition was for them to continue bearing this testimony and leading the people to do likewise. Joshua knew that affluency lends itself to apathy. The people poured out their hearts to God when they were in Egypt. The people cried out to God for help when Pharaoh's army was in hot pursuit. The people fell on their knees and depended on God to overthrow the Canaanites, so they could inherit the

Joshua knew that affluency lends itself to apathy.

Promised Land. But now they are there; now they enjoy the pleasures of this good land; now they finally have a home and a land; now they are well established. It has been my experience and observation that it is easier to depend on God and stay committed to Him in the bad times rather than the good times. But Jesus is the God of all times. He is not a way of life - He is life! Therefore, we must allow Him to keep us "glued" to Himself in all situations and predicaments.

The fourth word from the Word is *conquest.* Joshua told his leadership team that staying "glued" to God would continue giving them the conquest. God's power meant that though Israel was outnumbered, it did not matter as long as they were obedient!

> "For the LORD hath driven out from before you great nations and strong: but as for you, no man hath been able to stand before you unto this day. One man of you shall chase a thousand: for the LORD your God, he it is that fighteth for you, as he hath promised you" (Joshua 23:9-10).

These verses remind me of two wonderful passages from Romans chapter eight:

> "...If God be for us, who can be against us?" (v. 31)

> "...in all these things we are more than conquerors through him that loved us" (v. 37).

The Will of God

Joshua exposes the will of God in two areas of our lives. The first area deals with our *fellowship with the Father.* The number one priority of our existence is to have fellowship with our heavenly Father. I am convinced beyond a shadow of a doubt that God desires to have fellowship with us more than we desire to fellowship with Him. I believe this is the thought behind Jesus' statement to Jerusalem right before His crucifixion:

> "O Jerusalem, Jerusalem, thou that killest the prophets, and stonest them which are sent unto thee, how often would I have gathered thy children together, even as a hen gathereth her chickens under her wings, and ye would not!" (Matthew 23:37)

I am convinced beyond a shadow of a doubt that God desires to have fellowship with us more than we desire to fellowship with Him.

Fellowship with God shows love for God because you fellowship with those you love. When you love someone, you want to spend time with that person. You enjoy times of intimacy with that special someone. Joshua already had prescribed what love for God looked like in Joshua 22:5:

- Walk in all of God's ways.
- Obey God's commands.
- Hold fast to Him.
- Serve God with all of one's heart and soul.

If the number one priority of my existence is to have fellowship with the Father, then what is the number two priority of my life? It is to *focus on my family.* He admonished the Israelites that they were not to marry people in the land of Canaan. Was Joshua prejudiced? No. His purpose was not because of racial prejudice but spiritual separation. This idea is reinforced in no uncertain terms in 2 Corinthians 6:14-17:

> "Be ye not unequally yoked together with unbelievers: for what fellowship hath righteousness with unrighteousness? and what communion hath light with darkness? And what concord hath Christ with Belial? or what part hath he that believeth with an infidel? And what agreement hath the temple of God with idols? for ye are the temple of the living God; as God hath said, I will dwell in them, and walk in them; and I will be their God, and they shall

be my people. Wherefore come out from among them, and be ye separate, saith the Lord, and touch not the unclean thing; and I will receive you."

God is not prejudiced. He desires for everyone to be saved and for no one to perish (2 Peter 3:9). However, He does not want His children to marry unbelievers. God made the home a priority way back in the Garden of Eden when He created Adam and Eve and instituted marriage.

It is God's design for the home to be the place of instruction and development. Therefore, it is not the school's responsibility to raise our children. Furthermore, it is not the church's fault when kids turn out bad. The church is to support, undergird and help in the process. But God never gave children to churches; He gave them to parents!

Dictators know that if they can weaken family ties they can win the people's total allegiance much easier. The government then becomes the undergirding, supporting factor in their lives.

Joshua saw both destructive problems and dreadful promises if the family alliance was scattered. He told his leaders that they would be driven out of the land by God if they married the pagan people in the land. This godly leader said they could "know for a certainty" heathen people would become:

"snares and traps unto you, and scourges in your sides, and thorns in your eyes" (Joshua 23:13).

Why is it that Joshua made such a big deal out of this? Because we become ensnared by the sin we tolerate!

It is my belief that if you can't be a good Christian at home, you can't be a good Christian anywhere. However, the opposite is true: If you can be a good Christian at home, you can be a good Christian anywhere! I want the people who know

We become ensnared by the sin we tolerate!

me the best to be the ones who are the most complimentary of me. I want my family to think more highly of me than anyone who hears me preach. As I have said, it's one thing to be a good preacher; but it's an entirely different thing to be a good husband, father, and now, grandfather.

The Ways of God

The fourth and last reminder that Joshua gives of God's blessings upon them deals with the ways of God. He tells them of the *faithfulness of God.* He lets them know that he is about to die, but he first wants to pass on the torch of God by encouraging them with the goodness and faithfulness of the Almighty:

> "...and ye know in all your hearts and in all your souls, *that not one thing hath failed* of all the good things which the LORD your God spake concerning you; all are come to pass unto you, and not one thing hath failed thereof." (Joshua 23:14, emphasis mine)

It really is true that Jesus never fails. Joshua was 110 years old and could testify of that. I am 47 years old; but I, too, share that testimony. Jesus has been so faithful! He has kept every promise! He has never let me down!

Joshua closes this vision-casting session to the new generation of leaders by dwelling on the *future with God.* The ways of God are truly faithful, but the ways of God also include a promising future. As great as God has been in the past, I am convinced that His greatest days are still yet future. The blessings of the past are an indicator of His future grace that will flow.

However, Joshua again cautions them to not transgress the ways of God. Although Joshua was a great military leader, he recognized Israel's greatest future threat was not military arsenal but a spiritual arsenal. Someone has well said, "As a nation, we have become technological giants and moral adolescents!" Do not be deceived by the devil into believing that America's economy will save us. God is not impressed with our economy; He is impressed with right living.

> "Righteousness exalteth a nation: but sin is a reproach to any people" (Proverbs 14:34).

Joshua certainly teaches us how to live godly in Christ Jesus so that we can pass the torch on to those who come behind us. You have the opportunity to run your race and carry your torch. Will you so run that you may pass your torch on to those waiting to receive it? Or will you disqualify yourself and have no flaming torch to pass on?

The Rest of Your Life

Jesus said, "...I am come that they might have life, and that they might have it more abundantly" (John 10:10). Jesus not only wants to give you life but *abundant* life. What are you doing with your life? Right now, you are either wasting it, spending it or investing it. And only you can determine which course to follow. We have all heard the old cliché: "I've got more time than money." But the late author Ernest Hemingway appropriately responded to that by his statement: "Time is the least thing we have of." Therefore, you need not seek more days in your life; but seek more life in your days!

Each of us should determine to live the rest of our lives so that we will produce fruit that remains (John 15:16). We cannot undo yesterday, but we can change the direction of our lives today to produce fruit tomorrow. Like a fruit tree, we do not produce fruit in every season. There are three seasons that each of us experiences in life.

The first is a time to *refresh*. This is the time when we are dormant as far as fruit producing is concerned and when we have the opportunity to evaluate our lives and inspect the fruit. We all must stop occasionally to ask: "What kind of fruit is my life producing?" "Am I satisfied with this fruit?" This is the winter season of life, a time to inspect.

The second season is a time to *refuel*. Because we have inspected and evaluated our lives, we now have clearer vision as to the purpose that will give our life direction. In this season of life, blossoms begin to appear on your branches and anticipation runs high as to the development of your life. This is a growing time when God prepares you for the coming harvest. This is the spring season of life, a time to inject.

The third season is a time to *refire*. It is during this season that you produce fruit, good fruit, fruit that remains, fruit that is enjoyed by all because "...every good tree bringeth forth good fruit" (Matthew 7:17). And people will know you by the fruit you produce. (Matthew 7:20) This is the summer season of life, a time to expect.

During the reign of Oliver Cromwell, the British government began to run low on silver coins. Lord Cromwell sent his men to the local cathedral to see if they could find any precious metal there. After investigating they reported, "The only silver we can find is in the statues of the saints standing in the corners." The radical soldier and statesman of England replied, "Good! We'll melt down the saints and put them in circulation!"

That brief, but direct, order states the essence of the practical goal of authentic Christianity and answers the question: "How should I live the rest of my life?" It is not rows of silver saints crammed into the corners of the cathedrals that will produce fruit that lasts but melted saints circulating through the mainstream of humanity!

As I live the rest of my life, I want it to be distinguished by eight characteristics.

Be a Man of Character
Proverbs 11:3 states, "The integrity of the upright shall guide them: but the perverseness of transgressors shall destroy them." Raymond Edman said, "To be torn unmercifully by external forces, and still to preserve one's inward integrity, is to know the discipline that endures." Even in times of great trial, it is our character that will guide us. Character has a way of burning through the modern-day teaching of situation ethics to give us a clear, concise answer - just as the bright morning sun burns away the early fog.

> "He that walketh uprightly walketh surely: but he that perverteth his ways shall be known" (Proverbs 10:9).

> *Character has a way of burning through the modern-day teaching of situation ethics to give us a clear, concise answer.*

As a young lawyer but yet a man of character, Abraham Lincoln was very selective as to the people he represented. After carefully listening to the details of a prospective client who sought his counsel, Lincoln responded: "You have a pretty good case in technical law but a pretty bad one in equity and justice. You will have to get someone else to represent you. I can't do it. All the time while persuading the jury I'd be thinking: 'Lincoln, you're a liar.'"

There are many businessmen who feel that the world is a

battlefield. They figure all is fair in love, war and business transactions. They practice "the end justifies the means" theory of life. If I come out on top, if I get the sale, if I make money and become a success, then I am to be considered a winner who endured the battle. There's just one problem with that: I will stand before Almighty God and give an account of the "means." God is not nearly as impressed with our "successes" as we are. However, He is greatly concerned about our character.

God is not nearly as impressed with our "successes" as we are.

You will recall that in Genesis 13 Abram (later changed to Abraham) and his nephew Lot had large herds and flocks so that "the land was not able to bear them, that they might dwell together: for their substance was great, so that they could not dwell together" (v. 6). Abraham decided to avoid the strife by parting ways and gave Lot the right to select the land he wanted first. As the elder of the two, it was customary for Abraham to select first. However, he was more interested in maintaining his character than in worldly gain. Lot, on the other hand, was not the least bit hesitant to select his land first. It would appear that he relished "success." The end result, however, was not favorable for Lot as he ended up in a land with sexual immorality and homosexual activity. God rained down fire upon the city. Lot escaped town; losing all he owned and having his wife look back on the city in disobedience to God's command "and she became a pillar of salt" (Genesis 19:26). It is evident that Mrs. Lot also had become fond of the world's wealth.

Abraham took the high road and was blessed of God. Genesis 17 records the results. God said to Abraham:

> "I will make my covenant between me and thee..." (v. 2).
>
> "I will make thee exceeding fruitful..." (v. 6a).
>
> "I will make nations of thee..." (v. 6b).
>
> "I will establish between me and thee and thy seed for an everlasting covenant..." (v. 7).
>
> "And I will give unto thee, and to thy seed after thee, the land wherein thou art a stranger..." (v. 8).

Character will make a man pure, but it also will make him profitable. Again, Proverbs 22:1 gives sound instruction:

> "A good name is more desirable than great riches; to be esteemed is better than silver or gold" (NIV).

Recently, I was asked to participate on a Drug Task Force put together by our local school system. I found it was somewhat easy to say what the kids were not supposed to do. It was quite a different thing to live our lives before them in an exemplary way. Many were offended when I stated that our kids would not clean up their act until we adults cleaned up ours. I asked the chairman of the committee what was the number one abused substance in America. Her reply: "Alcohol." I responded by asking how our kids were going to get off drugs when we were sipping drinks in our homes. Adults say they drink only *socially;* our young people respond by stating they only smoke pot *recreationally.* What our young people need are godly men and women who will be persons of character!

I do not want to hide what I do or say around my daughters or grandchildren. I want them to know me as a man of character. I want my lifestyle to be consistent whether I'm preaching at church, shopping at the mall or golfing at the course.

You see, when Jesus Christ came into my heart, He started molding me into a man of character because He changed my "want-to's." I am highly concerned about folks who profess Jesus but whose lifestyle has never been altered. When Jesus placed character in my heart, He gave me a great companion. Character is good company when you turn out the lights at night, for it is then that you live only with God and yourself. It is good company when you get up the next morning, look into the mirror and face the real you. It makes for good company at the office when your peers respect you for who you are. Abraham Lincoln, the most embattled president our country has known, once stated, "When I lay down the reigns of this administration, I want to have one friend left. And that friend is inside of me." This great man knew the value of character.

Character is good company when you turn out the lights at night, for it is then that you live only with God and yourself.

Be a Man of Faithfulness
Faithfulness is too often viewed with a past-tense perspective. We look at a person's past and see how faithful they have been; but I want my faithfulness to be active today, and I want my faithfulness to endure until I breathe my last

breath. It is wonderful to have a faithful past, but our faithfulness also should have a present and future tense to it. The whole course of our lives should be lived in faithfulness.

Solomon was a faithful man. He asked for wisdom from God in order to rule the nation of Israel in lieu of riches and wealth. He was faithful in building the Temple. Yet, toward the end of his life, the Bible says:

> "For it came to pass, when Solomon was old, that his wives turned away his heart after other gods: and his heart was not perfect with the LORD his God, as was the heart of David his father. For Solomon went after Ashtoreth the goddess of the Zidonians, and after Milcom the abomination of the Ammonites. And Solomon did evil in the sight of the LORD, and went not fully after the LORD, as did David his father" (1 Kings 11:4-6).

Solomon had a faithfulness that had a past but was void of a present and future. The key is not how faithful we have been but how faithful we will be.

Professional sports have a Hall of Fame which honors persons for their past accomplishments. The Bible records a Hall of Fame in Hebrews 11 that lists those whose faithfulness spanned their lifetime. Solomon is not recorded in the Bible Hall of Fame. One may argue that he was the wisest man who ever lived and, therefore, deserved such an honor. However, the Holy Spirit moved the writer of Hebrews to list only those who were faithful to the end. Wisdom, as much as we all need it, is not one of the qualifications to enter the Bible Hall of Fame. The only criteria that must be met is faithfulness!

Moses was such a man. Hebrews chapter 11 mentions his faithfulness on five occasions:

"By faith Moses..." (v. 23).
"By faith Moses..." (v. 24).
"By faith he..." (v. 27).
"Through faith he..." (v. 28).
"By faith they..." (v. 29).

Moses was inducted into the Bible Hall of Fame because he, like the others who are listed, knew the disciplines of durability.   In Hebrews 11:27 we find two key words that described this great man of God: "...he endured...." The word *endured* could be translated "he kept right on going." Wouldn't you like to have that said about you? He was faithful when he was twenty years old; he was faithful when he was forty years old; he is now sixty-five years old; and he's still faithful and going right on. We should each desire for our life to be characterized by the fact that we keep on going. The phrase "he endured" encompasses the idea that he persevered; he was resolute; he held staunchly to his purpose; he never flinched. What a testimony! So many people waver in their convictions that we often ask: "Well, how is so-and-so doing *now*?"   Faithfulness is not a test of intelligence or strength or beauty or eloquence; it is a test of will. Somewhere in the deep recesses of our souls we must resolve within ourselves that we will live faithful and will stay faithful.

Faithfulness is not a test of intelligence
or strength or beauty or
eloquence; it is a test of will.

Understand the Significance of One

God has always underscored individual involvement, and He still does! You have one solitary life and only one. We need to rid ourselves of thinking that our one little contribution does not matter. Your one little contribution may be like that of the widow who dropped her two small coins into the offering plate. She did not give a large sum of money, but yet she was the only one recognized by the Lord Jesus that day. It is refreshing to know that the Almighty God of Heaven recognizes our small, but faithful, contributions.

The significance of one may be seen in the following questions and answers:

- How many were chosen by God to confront Pharaoh and lead the Exodus? One.

- How many prophets were called to stand before wicked King Ahab and predict a drought? One.

- How many were needed to confront adulterous David and bring him to his knees in repentance? One.

- How many sheep were lost and became the object of concern to the Shepherd? One.

- How many did it take to help the victim who was mugged on the Jericho Road? One.

- How many did it take to stand up and preach on the day of Pentecost when 3,000 were saved? One.

- And how many did it take to die for our sins and redeem us to God? One.

Edward Everett Hale, noted author who was the U. S. chaplain in the early 1900's, once said,

> *"I am only one*
> *But I am still one.*
> *I cannot do everything,*
> *But still I can do something.*
> *And because I cannot do everything,*
> *I will not refuse to do something that I can do."*

The significance of one is seen in history:

- 1645 - One vote gave Oliver Cromwell control of England.

- 1776 - One vote gave America the English language instead of German.

- 1845 - One vote brought the territory of Texas into the Union.

- 1868 - One vote saved President Andrew Johnson from being removed from office.

- 1875 - One vote changed France from a monarchy to a republic.

- 1923 - One vote gave Adolph Hitler control of the Nazi Party.

Does one make a difference? The answer is a definite yes! We live in a time when significance is equated with bigness. If it isn't big, then it isn't considered important. This, however, is not godly thinking. The prophet Zechariah asked the question: "For who hath despised the day of small things?..." (4:10). God never works big things out of you until He first works small things into you. In Matthew 25 Jesus taught us about the greatest thing that will ever be: Heaven. He used the parable of the talents to teach us about being faithful in the small things and, therefore, receiving the opportunity to do even more.

> "...Well done, good and faithful servant; thou hast been faithful over a few things, I will make thee ruler over many things: enter thou into the joy of thy lord" (v. 23).

God never works big things out of you until He first works small things into you.

There is such a sea of people in this old world going in the wrong direction that many think their voices are muddled and unheard. Satan has sold us that lie long enough. The Church of Jesus Christ has a voice that needs to be heard and should be heard. There is significance in one who gives the clear, clarion call of the Word of God; and we need to no longer be intimidated by the devil and his crowd. We need to stand up and be counted!

Know the Difference between Outstanding vs. Valuable
The National Basketball Association gives the Most Valuable Player award to the person who is most valuable to the team. One year Magic Johnson won over Michael Jordan. The reason given was that while Michael was outstanding, Magic was valuable. The MVP award takes into consideration individual performance but also the ability to inspire and involve one's teammates, encouraging and enabling them to excel.

I do not want our church to be known as a place to just go and hear Johnny Hunt. It is not my desire for our dear church to be built upon outstanding star performers. I want to be valuable to our church; I want our staff members to be valuable to our church; I want everyone in our church to be valuable to the church. I am not looking for a collection of star performers who put on a show each Sunday. You see, we are not in the entertainment business; we are in the business of impacting people's lives so that they can be fruit producers and fruit reproducers. It is amazing how Jesus took a group of twelve men - none of whom were stars - and so impacted our world with them that we still see the effects of today.

The Apostle Paul, expounding on this fact, wrote:

> "For ye see your calling, brethren, how that not many wise men after the flesh, not many mighty, not many noble, are called: But *God hath chosen* the foolish things of the world to confound the wise; and *God hath chosen* the weak things of the world to confound the things which are mighty; And base things of the world, and things which are despised, *hath God chosen*, yea, and things which are not, to bring to nought things that are" (1 Corinthians 1:26-28, emphasis added).

God, in His great wisdom, did not choose the show horses. He chose us workhorses!

God, in His great wisdom, did not choose the show horses. He chose us workhorses!

I like to involve as many people as possible in our church ministries. We often select only a few "top-round draft choices" to do the work, hoping to put in place those who can be outstanding in ministry. This type of mentality may cause us to miss some that *God hath chosen* to serve in the ministries of our churches for His honor and glory. We must remember that we are there to glorify Him, not self. We must constantly ask ourselves: "Whose kingdom are we building?" Therefore, it should not be our pursuit to have an outstanding ministry but to have a valuable ministry.

I often hear preachers who profess spending forty or fifty hours of study per sermon. I would like to say to them: "That is good, but how much time did you spend with your people this week?" You see, I want to be a good preacher. I want to preach a prepared message. I want to feed the sheep of God when they come to church on Sunday. But I also want to get out there and touch them and add value to their lives. I do not want to be so outstanding in the pulpit that I cannot be valuable to my people individually.

Many men are truly outstanding in their field of work, but often I receive calls and letters from their wives who say they add no value to their home. They have learned to be outstanding professionally without being valuable personally. We have become a nation that so strives for the big that we have forgotten the little. Greatness comes by doing small things exceptionally well. Doing big things may make you outstanding, but doing the little things will make you valuable.

Doing big things may make you outstanding, but doing the little things will make you valuable.

We feel we can gain the confidence of the world if we can pull off the big things. But when we neglect our families, we lose the greatest source of confidence that is at our disposal outside of our relationship with Jesus Christ. When one has the knowledge that his family loves and respects him, he will abound with confidence. Is that to say that he will ever be devoid of weaknesses? Absolutely not. What then is the difference? Confident people neutralize their handicaps by focusing on their strengths. As Christians our strength is Jesus Christ. We need to focus on Him, not on ourselves. Peter is a classic example. He asked for and received permission from the Lord to walk on the water. As you know, he was doing just fine until he took his eyes off Jesus and put them on his circumstances. At that moment he began to sink. Our confidence is in Him! Paul stated in Philippians 1:6:

> "Being confident of this very thing, that he which hath begun a good work in you will perform it until the day of Jesus Christ."

Be God's Man in Reality, Not Just in Image

Many people have a great image and look so fine. They are impressive and project themselves well in the public eye. But deep down there is little character. When it comes to show, their gauge reads "full;" but when it comes to substance, the gauge indicates "empty."

Our Christian society has erroneously substituted worldly success for authenticity. That kind of success has nothing to do with being a genuine man or woman of God in reality. We have replaced fame for faith, glamour for genuineness, popularity for prudence and riches for resolve. These words are not synonymous. We need a new understanding today of what being a real follower of the Lord Jesus Christ is all about.

We have the wrong heroes today. Many of America's teens have plastered posters of athletes and rock stars all over their bedroom walls when many of these so-called stars have beaten their wives, neglected their children and taken drugs. Their lives in no way represent an exemplary lifestyle. You take away their singing or athletic ability, place them in a common man's job; and this same person will be called a disgrace. You see, he may look good, present a favorable image but have no real substance or quality in his life that would be admired by anyone.

I think of Elvis Presley. He was handsome and talented. His smile and wink melted hearts the world over. The handkerchief he used to wipe the perspiration from his brow was a most valued commodity - even to the point that women would faint upon catching it as he threw it out into the audience. This man seemed to have it all. Yet he lived in a nightmare world of depression, despair and massive doses of drugs. He was lonely even in the crowds. Many say he was successful; but if he was, then I want none of it.

Being God's man in reality is not just a challenge for the rich and famous; it's also a struggle for the poor and unpopular. The truth is that we all want to be something that we're not. That's not bad in and of itself. However, we need to allow Jesus to change who we are and not camouflage who we really are. Two biblical examples illustrate this truth for us.

The first example is Adam and Eve as recorded in Genesis 3. After their sin they made fig leaves to hide their nakedness and sinfulness. They hid from God and then blamed someone else for their sin. Adam blamed Eve, and Eve blamed the serpent. They were clearly playing the image game. They did not want to admit to the reality of their sinfulness.

The second example is the story of Ananias and Sapphira in Acts 5. They sold a piece of property and gave some of the money to be used in helping those within the church that were less fortunate. But being so concerned with their image and wanting to boast that they had sacrificed as Barnabas had (Acts 4:36-37), they decided to lie about the amount given, implying to the early church that they were giving it all. Now it needs to be understood that they were not required to give it all. They had the option of giving part of it or none of it (vs. 3-4). But desiring to be godly in image rather than in reality, they chose to lie about the amount. Because they "lied unto God" (vs. 4), they both dropped dead upon being confronted by the Apostle Peter.

Three truths from these biblical illustrations are:

- Image is short-lived.

- God is not impressed with our image.

- Reality will eventually surface.

One writer stated, "The safest route to follow is Authenticity Avenue - walled on either side by Accountability and Vulnerability." Born-again believers in Jesus Christ ought to be involved with others who will help them be real and accountable. This is one reason I strongly believe in Sunday School. In those small groups, people can stand with each other, encourage each other, pray for each other and hold each other accountable.

Mark Twain said, "Everyone is a moon and has a dark side

which he never shows to anybody." We need to let the Lord clean our lives; we need to let Him scrub that dark side of our lives so we can be the people we ought to be.

It's amazing how children have the unique ability to see through image. I think it's because they have not been so conditioned as adults to strive for image. If we put up such an image as to not see our real selves, then how will we ever detect "imaging" in others? So if your vision is getting a little blurry and your morale is beginning to fade, realize by the grace of God that you can be what He wants you to be in reality. Let's be real at home, at work, at church and in the marketplace.

Have a Good, Private Walk with Jesus Christ

This truth seems to be so simple that it is almost overlooked. Again, life is made up of the small, simple things. The quality of our lives will be in direct proportion to the attention given to the basics of life. Nothing is more basic to the child of God than a personal time with Him each day. If you don't take time to be holy, you won't possess the stuff that makes a great Christian.

> *The quality of our lives will be in direct proportion to the attention given to the basics of life.*

I have found that I can be no better publicly than I have been privately. We will never stand tall on our feet until we have first knelt down on our knees.

The most important thing in my life is not my messages from

the pulpit; it's my moments in the prayer closet. As in any relationship, the more time spent with that person, the better acquainted you become. To know God intimately means I must spend time with Him. There are no shortcuts, no instant pills to swallow - just a day-by-day relationship as I sit at Jesus' feet.

In this way I will not only experience real victory in my life, but I will possess real joy in my life - joy that comes from within, and is not determined by the external circumstances of the world.

Know the Things I Wish to Accomplish
I had to ask myself what I really wanted from life. Most people go through life and never ask this most vital question. We get so caught up in a rat-race world and a society seeking materialism that we have been conditioned to believe that accomplishment in life is determined by our accumulation of things. Jesus said in Luke 12:15:

> "Take heed, and beware of covetousness: for a man's life consisteth not in the abundance of the things which he possesseth."

Therefore, we need to ask ourselves the right question.

- Wrong Question: "What can I accumulate?"

- Right Question: "What can I accomplish?"

Here are four things I would like to accomplish in my life.

1. Cultivate relationships.

My spiritual gift is "hanging out." I love getting to know people and building relationships with them. I have been told that a pastor of a large church cannot personally pour his life into people or be accessible to the people. I just don't believe that! God calls pastors to shepherd the flock, and I've noticed that you cannot shepherd your sheep by proxy. Shepherds in the Bible were always with their sheep. Here are some ways I go about cultivating relationships.

- I eat with twenty people each Wednesday night at our church.

- My wife and I recently took several Sunday nights and had our children and youth in our home for food and fellowship. Immediately after church, we would load up all the kindergarten children in the church bus and haul them over to the house and "hang out" with them. After a couple of hours, we'd pile them all back on the bus and deliver them to the church parking lot where their parents picked them up. The following Sundays we would have the first graders, then the second graders, etc., until we "graduated" with our seniors. We are now in the process of doing the same with all our adult Sunday School classes.

- There's hardly a work day that I don't have lunch with someone.

- As often as I can, I take people with me when I travel.

2. Build memories.

While on sabbatical leave, I visited the church that my brother, Norman, pastors. He shared with the congregation how I started witnessing to him after I got saved. He was a church member, but there was no change in his life. He kept telling me that he was a good churchman, but I insisted that when

Jesus came into my life, there was a distinct change that took place. The church we attended passed a book around, and people would write down their prayer requests. One night we passed the book around and Norman was the last to receive it. He decided to scan through it since no one else needed to write a request in the book. He noticed that for several weeks I had listed his name and asked people to pray for his salvation. God used that to place him under conviction, and he was converted. That is a memory that he or I will never forget.

Several years ago I promoted a crusade in a local stadium, and a young man named Steve Flockhart literally ran down the aisle during the invitation to receive Christ. Since then, God has allowed me to baptize him, disciple him, hire him as a staff member and ordain him to the Gospel ministry. He is now pastoring. I have been to his church and preached in worship services there on several occasions. We now share some great memories with each other.

3. A deliberate pursuit of ministries that will yield eternal dividends.

Our church is involved with many churches in America and around the world. This past year our church conducted mission projects in 20 countries: Argentina, Benin, Bosnia, Brazil, China, Costa Rica, Croatia, France, Hungary, Indonesia, Mexico, Puerto Rico, Russia, Singapore, Slovakia, Thailand, Turkey, Uganda, Ukraine and Uzbekistan. Our church supports these world mission efforts with both money and people. Short-term mission endeavors this year involved 371 people with a total gift support of $652,000. In addition, 30 missionaries and other mission churches and ministries were underwritten by a "Faith Promise Budget" of $489,000, which is pledged above and beyond the tithe. I want my ministry and our church's ministries to impact the Kingdom of God by seeing people get saved and developed into Christlikeness.

4. Keep my work fun.

I understand that the work God has called me to is honorable and valuable, but I also want it to be enjoyable. This principle is not deep, but it sure is needed!

I Don't Want to Ever Quit

I am convinced that when we who are leading quit, it gives others a reason for quitting. Quitting breeds quitting. When you give up, it gives others a reason to give up. Even as you can *inspire* others, you also can *expire* others.

No one wants to quit when things are going good. But every now and then God may send some trial your way to mature you, to grow you up. If we get discouraged and quit, then we have quit over the very thing that God wanted to use to mature us! What does God want us to do? He would have us to go on, to continue with Him in the good times as well as the bad. He has promised us in Galatians 6:9:

> "And let us not be weary in well doing: for in due season we shall reap, if we faint not."

We are to be like the oyster that produces pearls as a result of irritation when the shell of the oyster is invaded by an alien substance - like a grain of sand. When that happens, all of the resources within the tiny, sensitive oyster rush to the irritated spot and begin to release healing fluids that otherwise would have remained dormant. By and by, the irritation is covered and turns into a beautiful pearl. Had there been no irritating interruption, there could have been no pearl. The Bible states it this way:

> "Consider it pure joy, my brothers, whenever you face trials of many kinds, because you know that the testing of your faith develops perseverance. Perseverance must finish its work so that you may be mature and complete, not lacking anything" (James 1:2-4, NIV).

You cannot go back and undo yesterday. You cannot eliminate yesterday's failures or erase her scars. But you can go on from here. You can start a new beginning today. Be encouraged — yesterday ended last night and is forever gone! You may be thinking: *But Johnny you don't know how I've blown it.* You're right, I don't know your failures and neither do you know mine, but God does! And He addresses that by asking five rhetorical questions in Romans eight:

> "If God be for us, who can be against us?" (v. 31)

> "He that spared not his own Son, but delivered him up for us all, how shall he not with him also freely give us all things?" (v. 32)

> "Who shall lay anything to the charge of God's elect? It is God that justifieth" (v. 33).

> "Who is he that condemneth? It is Christ that died, yea rather, that is risen again, who is even at the right hand of God, who also maketh intercession for us" (v. 34).

> "Who shall separate us from the love of Christ? shall tribulation, or distress, or persecution, or famine, or nakedness, or peril, or sword?" (v. 35)

Paul concludes this rich chapter with a most uplifting admonition:

"Nay, in all these things we are more than conquerors through him that loved us. For I am persuaded, that neither death, nor life, nor angels, nor principalities, nor powers, nor things present, nor things to come, Nor height, nor depth, nor any other creature, shall be able to separate us from the love of God, which is in Christ Jesus our Lord" (Romans 8:37-39).

The fact is you can begin "building your spiritual resume" today. God's grace will enable you and empower you for this purpose. As Paul exhorted young Timothy:

"For God hath not given us the spirit of fear; but of power, and of love, and of a sound mind. Be not thou therefore ashamed *of the testimony of our Lord . . .*" (2 Timothy 1:7-8, emphasis mine).

Give the rest of your life to building a spiritual resume that will allow your testimony to outlast you.

Notes

Chapter One: *Out of the Poolroom*
1. *Just As I Am.*
Words, Charlotte Elliott, 1834. Tune WOODWORTH, William B. Bradbury, 1849.

2. *O Why Not Tonight?*
Eliza Reed, 1794-1867, alt.; J. Calvin Bushey.

Chapter Two: *The Making of a Testimony*
1. *I Surrender All.*
Words, Judson W. Van DeVenter, 1896. Tune SURRENDER, Winfield S. Weeden, 1896.

2. *Rescue the Perishing.*
Words, Fanny J. Crosby, 1869. Tune RESCUE, William H. Doane, 1869.

3. *When We All Get to Heaven.*
Words, Eliza E. Hewitt, 1898. Tune HEAVEN, Emily D. Wilson, 1898.

Chapter Six:: *God's Others*
1. *Stand Up, Stand Up for Jesus.*
Ephesians 6:10-20. Words, George Duffield, Jr., 1858. Tune GEIBEL, Adam Geibel, 1901.